Limbo
on the
Yalu

May God Bless you always
with good health & wealth

Sincerely
Ted Sprouse

Limbo
on the
Yalu . . .
and Beyond!

by Robert J. Berens

Southern Heritage Press
St. Petersburg, Florida

SOUTHERN HERITAGE PRESS, INC.
P.O. BOX 10937
ST. PETERSBURG, FLORIDA 33733
800-282-2823
WWW.SOUTHERNHERITAGEPRESS.COM

Cover photo of the Korean War Memorial
by George G. Kundahl, Alexandria, VA.
Cover design by Byron L. Kennedy III

FOREWORD

This is the story of Teddy R. Sprouse, an ordinary citizen born and raised in the Middle West. He was a soldier, a noncommissioned officer, who became involved in the early days of the war in Korea. Captured in the fighting, he spent almost three years as a prisoner of war. The horror of this experience — Robert Berens calls it a life in limbo — turned into a trauma of psychological problems when Sprouse returned home after the Armistice of 1953. The unsettling condition persisted over the years until Sprouse, finally, with help of the Veterans Administration, won his way back to normality.

Berens's narrative starts slowly but builds through an increasing intensity to almost unbearable scenes of breakdown. His account is sombre as well as inspirational. It is a personal odyssey to mental health. Historians and other writers have rarely focused on this post-war aberration that struck many Korean War survivors. It is good to have Berens' interesting and highly readable work to remind us of the difficulties imposed on those who were in limbo during the Korean War a half century ago.

Martin Blumenson

Dedicated to loved ones who also serve. . .
by waiting.
R.J.B.

Prologue

At the outset I expected to find the life of Teddy R. (Ted) Sprouse uncomplicated—except that he had been a prisoner of war in North Korea for some thirty-three months. After all, he was born in tiny Drakesville, Iowa, on September 24, 1927, the fourth child of Charles ("Charlie") and Ida May (Robinson) Sprouse. Indeed, the Sprouses were ordinary people living in an ordinary state at an ordinary time.

However, singularity entered Ted Sprouse's life early on. First, the Great Depression soon engulfed the Sprouses and just about everyone else during the 1930s. Navigating an uncertain economy was tough for this family that approached an even dozen. For two adults and nine surviving children to get by in an era of self-reliance and recurrent joblessness necessitated everybody pitching in.

Second, Ted Sprouse was a good athlete. His baseball skills were evident from the beginning, and baseball would be the one big recreation in his youth. Thus, Ted's formative years were spent working or playing baseball.

In the meantime, war clouds gathered on distant horizons during the 1930s. Although midwesterners were isolationist to the core, eventually they would be drawn into a conflagration spreading throughout the world. And wars and threats of wars would linger over the next half century. The Sprouses would be involved tragically in two of them—World War II and the Korean Conflict.

In a metaphysical sense the times conditioned young Ted Sprouse, fostering qualities he would need in cruel and wrenching days ahead. Indeed, Ted matured with a deep sense of responsibility, a dogged determination and a predictability in character that would enable him to endure his limbo on the banks of the Yalu River—and in the aftermath. So, in unexpected ways the life of Teddy R. Sprouse was exceptional—truly!

I
EARLY YEARS

Only two hundred people lived in Drakesville, Iowa, when Ted Sprouse was born. Six miles away was Bloomfield, seat of Davis County. With a population of over two thousand, Bloomfield had a hospital, high school and stores to serve needs of surrounding farm families. Southeastern Iowa, an agriculture area of rolling lands, was a good place to raise a large family on modest income.

The Sprouse family was large, nearly a dozen survivors in all, and the income was modest. Charlie Sprouse sheared sheep, an occupation that took him beyond the limits of Drakesville in pursuit of the flocks. Charlie would pack his work clothes and tools and tour northern Iowa, Illinois, Wisconsin, Minnesota, the Dakotas and Nebraska. He would return to Drakesville and his family on nights he was within striking distance. Other times he made it back on weekends.

Ida May tended her brood of four boys and five girls. The eldest boy Don was born in 1922. Then at more or less regular intervals there followed Rex, Betty, Ted, Lois, Keith (who died shortly after birth), Shirley, Mary Jane, Kyle and Karen. The Sprouse children were "well brought up," as the saying went.

Large families were not unusual in farm country, since offspring could work in the fields and on crop-related tasks. Needs were based on essentials: comfortable home, healthy diet and adequate clothing. Children did not question parental authority. As Betty Sprouse Zaerr

1

The Sprouse Family, taken September 24, 1943, just before Rex went into the service. Back row: Betty, Ted, Rex, Ray and Lois. Front row: Dad, Shirley, Kyle, Mary Jane, Karen and Mom.

was to say much later, "Respecting your parents and elders was a way of life—not a choice!" They made their own fun, playing hide and seek, tag, Red Rover, and sleigh riding. On weekends the children attended Sunday School at the local Christian church.

Citizens of Drakesville were neighborly and always willing to help out; however, the Sprouses believed in helping themselves. The younger children helped around the home while older ones helped Charlie "tie wool" or shear sheep. Ida managed a huge garden, including space borrowed from a neighbor. She grew every kind of vegetable and popcorn for treats. At harvest, Ida would turn up the root crops with a spade fork while children barehandedly dug potatoes, carrots, onions, parsnips and so forth out of loosened soil.

Certain crops had to be preserved and it was not unusual for the Sprouses to put up a thousand quarts of tomatoes, green beans, sauerkraut, pickles and peas in a year. At times little hands shriveled from scrubbing Mason jars and little fingers hurt from shelling popcorn by hand. But there was a pleasant side too. Sitting in front-porch sunlight shelling peas and snapping beans were times for talking about life and lighthearted things.

The Sprouse family was not poor, really. Ida saw to that, of course. She was a genius at improvising and affectionate in handling offspring. Shirley recalled, "We had no money then, but I was never hungry. I always had clean clothes to wear—and I always felt loved." Whereas, Charlie was given to bragging about the boys, Ida was not so inclined. When someone complimented the girls, Ida would say, "Pretty is as pretty does." Nonetheless, all sensed Ida was intensely proud of them.

Downtown Drakeville, Iowa, circa 1943, (population 200).

There was a drawback to living in Drakesville, however. There was no high school, so children had to go to Bloomfield for secondary education. There were no school buses in those days, so sometimes the Sprouse children caught a ride, sometimes they walked, and sometimes they stayed home and worked. After one year of high school, Ted Sprouse decided he had enough education.

At sixteen years of age, Ted stood 5'10" tall and weighed 170 pounds. Hard work and athletics had hardened his frame and toughened his mind. Then, too, he had been around. Ted often accompanied his father and Rex on sheep-shearing trips and he knew how to wrestle lambs into position and deftly clip away the wool. He also learned how to get along with people; Ted could talk with anybody. He could make do with only necessities and still be contented. Ted Sprouse grew up early—he had to!

Sheepshearing trips took Ted through drought-impaired areas in the upper midwest. The Dakotas, Nebraska and Kansas had been bone dry in the 1930s and were just coming out of the doldrums. Livestock tended to be undernourished, as did many of the people. Children in tattered clothing were commonplace. Wages Charlie received could be in the form of barter or cash—or skipped altogether. By comparison, the Sprouses were "pretty well off." Besides, Sprouses had diversions to lift their spirits.

Since he was not attending high school, Ted played baseball on an independent team. One advantage Ted had was that his father had been an excellent player. So Ted not only sheared sheep with his father, but he learned baseball from him as well. In fact, Ted eventually took over from his father as team catcher.

Ted became a good receiver in every sense of the word. He learned to handle pitchers and throw out runners straying too far from the bag. Ted liked catching because it was the most active role on the field. Not only did the catcher call pitches, but to a great extent he was in charge. With full view of the field, he would adjust positions of fielders according to called pitches. He could set up plays and frustrate the opposition's tactics and strategy. Yes, a catcher was responsible and he could play mind games, both of which appealed to Ted Sprouse.

Although Ted and his father excelled in baseball, the others were by no means unnoticed. Be it a backyard game, community fundraiser, or neighborly get-together, Sprouses would be involved. The whole gang usually ended up back at Ida's house. True, most would be her offspring to begin with, but Ida was always tolerant and resourceful with friends. She had a special recipe for popcorn, one that guests would beg their mothers to copy. Ida's secret was that she used bacon grease as shortening, which gave the popcorn a peppery taste that was uniquely appealing.

The Great Depression ebbed in the farm belt at the turn of the decade, somewhat later than in industrial areas to the east. Rains had returned to parched farms and prices were rising. Then, too, government programs paid farmers for "banking" soil, or selling crops into government storage at a reasonable price. Of course, there was another reason for the improving economy—war!

Adolph Hitler had set off World War II in Europe and the Allies were bidding for American weapons and products. And the conflict was not confined to Europe. Japan was fighting China and had designs on the whole Southwest Pacific. A wary United States Government passed the Selective Service Act in 1940, which placed a one-year military obligation on able-bodied men. Don Sprouse was among the first to register for the draft.

In the meantime, wool-production business picked up significantly. Charlie Sprouse and his sons were in big demand, especially at the slaughterhouse. In Dubuque, for example, there were 100,000 lambs annually to be sheared of their valuable coats. Then ninety days later, when lambs' coats had regained the appropriate thickness, the entire hide was harvested to be made into sheepskin jackets for pilots and other servicemen exposed to cold temperatures. Sheep shearing was an essential wartime occupation beyond a doubt.

Young men began leaving for the military in driblets at first, but after Pearl Harbor the flow became a river. Don, called up in early 1942, was found unfit for military service and sent home. A year later, Rex was drafted and sent to Fort Riley, Kansas, for training. The following spring he arrived in the British Isles for the Normandy invasion.

After D-Day, June 6, 1944, Charlie and Ida Sprouse followed the war by listening to the radio. Shirley and Mary Jane would wake each morning to the somber tones of radio commentators speaking in generalities about crucial battles as the Allies fought their way off the beaches. There was no way of gleaning how Rex was faring; however, something ominous emanated across the air waves.

Rex survived the invasion and fighting through the hedgerows of western France. When Allied troops reached Saint Lo, the Sprouses felt some relief. The invasion no longer was in doubt, and no news of Rex was surely good news. Disturbing, though, were reports of heavy casualties as the Allies advanced across France. Paris fell on August 25th, an encouraging sign.

Rex's unit, the 90th Infantry Division, swung past Paris, through Reims, across the Meuse River and beyond. Surely, the Germans would give up soon, now that Germany itself was threatened.

When the telegram arrived on September 10, 1944,

the whole town of Drakesville soon knew that Rex had been killed. Friends flocked to the Sprouse home to express sympathy. For the first time ever, family and friends saw Ida break down. Shirley believes a special bond existed between Rex and his mother, making the loss even more traumatic for her.

Rex had been a shy lad, quiet and considerate. His need for reassurance and affection appealed to his mother, naturally. Then, too, there would be no funeral, no burial, no occasion for an outpouring of grief that would facilitate closure.

On that sad evening, Lois took younger siblings for a stroll. They ambled quietly about the town square, recalling how they had played there in happier times. Mary Jane, nine years old, said, "I wish everyone would go away so that Mom'll stop crying."

Seventeen-year-old Ted seemed to bear up best. But it was a brave front he presented to others. "The bottom dropped out of my life," he said. "Rex and I were very close. We both went with dad on those sheep-shearing trips, one always helping the other. I couldn't let on how much I hurt because I had to be the strong one. But I never got over Rex's death, not to this day!"

Adding to misery was Don's having been found fit for military service after a second physical exam. He had just married and was training at Fort Riley. Surely, he would be sent overseas soon. What would happen to him? Might he also be killed—or maimed? The Army had a "last-surviving-son" policy by then, but with Ted and Kyle still at home the Sprouses did not qualify.

The family's concern was well founded, for Don was rushed to Europe upon completion of infantry training. The fighting was then at its peak as the Allies resolutely ground down Hitler's troops. The Sprouse family rallied around Don and his wife; what else could they do? Don did survive and when the war ended in May 1945, he remained in Europe on occupation duty and returned to Drakesville in 1946.

Although Rex's remains were never repatriated, he was memorialized at home nonetheless. The family received his dog tags—chips of metal stamped with his name, rank, serial number, blood type and religious preference—and an American flag. More soothing was a contribution from Ida's brother, Charley, who cross-bred flowers. Charlie created a unique gladiola, a blend of orange, peach and white that he named the "Rex." Thereafter, in her yard Ida grew Rex gladiolas near a big rock with her son's name and dates of his birth and death painted thereon.

Rex was memorialized in yet another way. When the $10,000 government insurance check came in 1944, Ida used the money to pay for their Drakesville home. Thus Rex left a "monument" of his own, a constant reminder to his survivors that he had once been with them—and in a sense would always be with them. In such fashion the Sprouses came to terms with grief.

When Japan surrendered in September 1945, everyone hoped that was the end of wars. Ironically, the end of fighting did not allay bitterness nor satisfy ambitions of the world's last great dictator, Joseph Stalin of the Soviet Union. At the outset of this "cold war," the Soviets seized territory in every direction while International Communism sought to undermine democracies everywhere. This disastrous turn of events had implications for everyone.

When he was called to Fort Snelling, Minnesota, in

late 1945 for a pre-induction physical, Ted Sprouse was deferred because of an irregular heartbeat. Although perplexed over the finding—Ted had never experienced any heart problems—he returned to shearing sheep, playing baseball and putting his future together. Ted Sprouse was content, even as he sought a way to spend the rest of his life.

"He was handsome with an easy-going personality," Shirley recalls. "He never wanted for friends, men or women. He was popular with everyone."

In several ways he was a father figure to siblings younger than himself. An empathic nature made Ted a good sounding board for anyone with adolescent challenges. In fact, he would go out of his way to snap someone out of a fit of depression. He also looked out for his marriage-eligible sisters. Once when a couple Bloomfield youths misbehaved around Shirley and Mary Jane, "Ted made believers out of those guys!" according to Shirley.

Charlie Sprouse boasted of Ted's prowess in sheep shearing and baseball, and well he should have. At the Iowa State Fair in 1946, Ted placed second in the sheep-shearing contest. Not bad considering the best shearers throughout the country had participated.

Ted was now regular catcher for the Drakesville All Stars, one of the best teams in southeast Iowa and northeast Missouri. Oren "Red" Jones was team manager—and more! "He used whatever leverage he could get to keep us out of trouble," Ted said in retrospect, "and I needed that at the stage in life I was going through. You know, beer and girls!"

So Ted had a streak of orneriness, but the vagaries Ted alluded to were common and fleeting. Besides, idyllic days in Southeast Iowa were drawing to a close. When

Ted was called back for a second physical, no sign of an irregular heartbeat appeared. He was declared physically fit for military service.

A carefree Ted Sprouse before he joined the army in 1948.

Ted Sprouse now faced a dilemma. If he were to be drafted, he would serve two years on active duty and six years in the reserves. Ordinarily, the reserve status wouldn't mean much; Ted would eventually slip into inactive status with little obligation. In 1948, however, Stalin cut off roads and railroads to Berlin, raising the spectre of war. President Harry Truman ordered an airlift to feed and supply Berliners. Any misstep could lead to a major war in Europe—if not the entire world! Clearly, the Cold War was not going away and Ted Sprouse would be liable for call up, even on an inactive status.

Another consideration entered into Ted's planning at that point. He had been dating Joanne Anderson from Centerville, and they were getting "serious." Of course, Ted couldn't support a wife at that stage, so he decided to enlist in the Regular Army for three years. Perhaps he could save some money, get his military obligation out of the way and be free of any future recall. Ultimately, he followed this course and reported on December 28th, 1948, to Fort Riley for military training—as had Rex and Don before him.

II
ANSWERING THE CALL

Ted Sprouse had his brothers in mind when he began basic training. Rex and Don had taken their military service in stride, doing so without complaint. Ted vowed he would do as well. He, too, was used to hard work and respectful of authority, so he had little difficulty the first twelve weeks. Next, he was sent to the 2nd Infantry Division (Indianhead) at Fort Lewis, Washington.

Ted took the scenic cross-country train ride to the Pacific northwest. He liked what he saw of Washingtonians. They were friendly, much as midwesterners were. It occurred to Ted that he would be fortunate, indeed, to spend a three-year hitch at Fort Lewis.

As a budding artilleryman, he was assigned to the 38th Field Artillery Battalion. Ted trained on the venerable 105-mm Howitzer, which had proven so reliable and effective during World War II. In fact, the version Ted worked with was the most popular artillery piece in the world. More than fifty countries

Ted Sprouse and pal Corporal Don Roe depart Ft. Riley for Ft. Lewis, WA in 1949.

11

M101A1 105-mm towed howitzer.

had bought the "105 How" for use in their armed forces. The "105" was towed by the standard Army two and a half-ton truck, the "deuce and a half."

As a neophyte in C Battery commanded by Captain Harold Kasko, Ted learned the various tasks of an artillery crewman. Although inspections and maintenance seemed overdone, he accepted the routine as necessary to ensure everything was combat ready—always! At the same time, he was surprised at how austere resources were; even ammunition, fuel and equipment essential to training were scarce. But here again, Ted Sprouse was used to doing without; therefore, he had a good idea of how to keep men and equipment functioning.

It wasn't long before soldiering became but a part of Ted's duties. Sports were popular in the peacetime Army, so Ted turned to playing baseball. Once his prowess was recognized, he was selected to play on the division artillery team (DIVARTY). With Ted catching, the team won seventy-two games and lost just three over the next fifteen months. One loss was a no hitter to the team from O'Neil Prison, which had some great players as inmates. Revealingly, prisoners managed just one hit themselves.

DIVARTY team's record did not go unnoticed. A New York Giant scout came by to observe several times, and he eventually invited Ted and a couple others to recruit-training camp in San Francisco in July 1949. The trip was a great adventure for the eager young catcher, who received tips from former major league players.

Ted held his own in drills and when the three-day camp ended he was told he was an "excellent receiver with a strong throwing arm." His hitting needed to be improved, but Ted believed he had picked up invaluable instruction that would certainly help. Encouraging, too, was word that the Giants wanted another look at Ted Sprouse when he completed military service.

During the course of his duties, Ted met a sergeant who had just returned from Europe. The sergeant had worked at American cemeteries and was familiar with those in France. When Ted told him about Rex, the sergeant explained how to locate Rex's burial site. Fur-

ther, Ted learned that Rex's remains would be returned to Drakesville for final burial at government expense if the family so requested.

When Ted wrote to authorities, he found out Rex had been killed in a mine blast along with others near Hayange, France. Ted discussed the matter with brother Don and both agreed they

Ted's brother Rex's grave in France.

Ted Sprouse, catcher for the Indianhead DIVARTY team in 1949.

could never be sure remains returned would be those of their brother. In an ensuing family discussion, all agreed it would be best to leave Rex buried at Lorraine American cemetery near St. Avold (Moselle), France.

Throughout 1949 and into the next year, Ted Sprouse enjoyed both soldiering and playing baseball. He was inspired by his marriage to Joanne Anderson in October 1949. Although they had talked of marrying several times, the ceremony itself was a spurious thing. While he was home on leave they sought out a Justice of the Peace in Centerville and were married with little fanfare. Two weeks after Ted's return to Fort Lewis, he rented an apartment in Tacoma and Joanne joined him.

It was a big change for Joanne, the youngest of eight siblings. She was nineteen at the time and had never ventured far from Centerville. Then, too, she had had no exposure to the military and its living style. Her education on life and the military would be harsh and erratic.

Ted was promoted to corporal shortly thereafter and the modest increase in pay was certainly welcomed. Then in the spring of 1950, he was made a buck sergeant. Hard work, positive thinking and leadership traits were paying off for Ted Sprouse. He was well liked by peers and superiors, and he was contentedly married. And then more good news! Their first child would be arriving in the fall of 1950. Indeed,

Catcher Ted Sprouse and DIVARTY pitcher, July 30, 1949

Ted considered himself most fortunate.

Ironically, with no warning everything changed!

The Sprouses had always been too caught up in making a living to pay much attention to history and foreign affairs. Typically, Ted had never given much thought to foreigners during his formative years. Europe and, especially, Asia were thousands of miles away and the United States was protected by two great oceans.

Of course, when Japan attacked Pearl Harbor on December 7, 1941, Ted agreed the United States had to defend itself. And when Hitler declared war on the United States, the country had no choice but to fight back. And when Rex was killed and Don endangered in Europe, Ted learned that defending America came at a price. But other families also lost loved ones, so the Sprouses nobly accepted their lot. Besides, if World War II ended war for generations, sacrifices probably had served a worthwhile purpose.

Such wishful thinking bore little fruit, however. On June 25th, 1950, all hell broke loose on the Korean Peninsula. Japan's World War II defeat had left a power vacuum in the Far East, one the Allies hoped would be filled peaceably. But the communists—despite enormous problems within North Korea, the Soviet Union and China—plunged ahead. Overnight, Korea became the focus of a very nervous world.

Hindsight disclosed miscalculations by everyone. After World War II, Korea had been divided at the 38th Parallel— an indefensible border ignoring geography altogether. (Map 1) The Soviet Union occupied the northern part and the United States the southern. In 1948, the Soviets withdrew, leaving Premier Kim Il Sung's communist government with a well trained and well equipped North Korean Peoples Army (NKPA). A year later, the United States withdrew, leaving President Syngman Rhee with a fledgling Republic of Korea Army (ROKA).

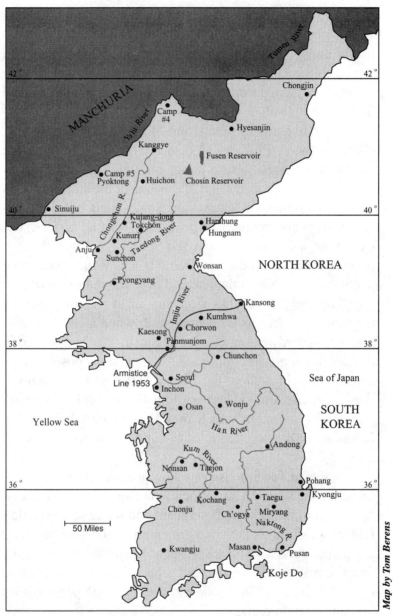

KOREAN BATTLEFIELD, 1950—53

17

Kim Il Sung liked the odds in this matchup. Without warning he sent the NKPA charging south to reunite the peninsula under communism. Caught short, the United States turned to the United Nations for a response to such blatant aggression. Sixteen other nations joined in, but the United States had to lead.

General Douglas MacArthur of World War II fame took charge, mustered forces and resources from throughout the Pacific and vowed to turn things around. The 2nd Infantry Division, Ted Sprouse's outfit, was one of the stateside units selected to reinforce MacArthur. So, in short order the leisurely pace and routines of peacetime became history. The Cold War had turned hot and Ted Sprouse, halfway through his enlistment, was now involved. Soon he would learn more about Asia and Korea than he had ever wanted to know.

The 2nd Infantry Division, similar to all Army units of the time, was seriously understrength when alerted for Korea. However, personnel specialists in Washington soon scraped up some five thousand "fillers" from posts, camps and stations throughout the United States and sent them to Fort Lewis. In similar fashion, logisticians scraped up supplies and equipment which they sent to Fort Lewis. The Indianhead Division had a lot of catching up to do in short order.

Sergeant Ted Sprouse was now an experienced noncommissioned officer (NCO). When new men joined C Battery, Ted was promoted to staff sergeant and made section chief. His responsibilities included nine men, a 105-mm howitzer and a deuce and a half truck. Even as he trained new arrivals, Sprouse readied his weapon and vehicle for overseas. He was up to the challenge and soon melded disparate personalities into an able gun crew.

Ted Sprouse and Pat Wieser at Yakima, Washington training center.

Officers were present, of course. A new lieutenant supervised preparations, but his primary job was to be a forward observer who adjusted artillery fires for a rifle company on the front lines. Sprouse worked more closely with a first lieutenant executive and gunnery officer, usually called the "XO." The XO supervised "laying " all six howitzers parallel so they fired as a unit, and he furnished fire direction data to guns during missions. But Sprouse actually ran the section, saw to it that crewmen fired off the 105-mm shells as ordered. Truly, noncommissioned officers were the "backbone of the army," the ones who accomplished all the essential tasks.

Then there was Sergeant First Class Don Cloud, a full-blooded Cherokee Indian from Oklahoma. Cloud had been pulled off ROTC duty at Virginia Military Institute and sent as a qualified cadreman to Fort Lewis. Since both were section chiefs in C Battery, Sprouse and Cloud worked together constantly. On a personal note, they hit it off from the beginning and became fast friends.

Don Cloud was impressive in every respect. He stood six feet tall and was a muscular 200 pounds. He was better educated than most NCOs, having taken college courses by extension. Cloud was also articulate, having polished his language skills as an ROTC instructor at Virginia Military Institute. Consequently, no one ever gave Cloud any guff.

Ted on his way to Korea in July, 1950

"Cloud taught me a lot," Sprouse recalls. "He was not just a good soldier but a genuine human being as well."

The mood of soldiers at Fort Lewis was mixed. Some were eager for a fight in Korea for pure adventure. Others were restrained for a variety of personal reasons. In Ted's case, he must now leave a pregnant wife to carry on alone.

Fundamentally, Ted had a job to do. He had made a bargain to be in the army for three years and it just happened that a war had occurred on his watch. He had no choice. So he put Joanne on a train back to Centerville, Iowa, and tried not to think of his parents suffering through the ordeal of yet another son in combat. He took out government life insurance and allotted all his pay but ten dollars a month to his wife.

All Indianheads shared one conviction as they readied for Korea: Americans would soon turn things around over there! After all, North Koreans had jumped on an ill-prepared, understrength South Korean army that was no match for them. But once GIs arrived on the scene, North Koreans would be put in their place—resoundingly! Indeed, Indianheads were confident as they readied to sail in July 1950.

In the meantime, employment of the 2nd Infantry Division was being debated in the halls of the Pentagon and elsewhere. General MacArthur wanted the division to invade Inchon on the west coast and sever the lifeline of hard-charging North Koreans. If MacArthur prevailed, the 2nd Infantry would land in Japan and prepare for the amphibious assault.

But fortunes of the hard-pressed UN forces worsened by the day—and resolved the immediate debate over the 2nd Infantry. The UN perimeter steadily shrank until survival of UN forces came into question. Therefore, the Indianhead Division was sent to Pusan without delay—lest all be lost! Troops for an Inchon landing would have to be assembled at a more propitious time.

First elements of the 2nd Infantry sailed from Seattle on July 17th. The 38th Field Artillery boarded the *USS Collins* in Tacoma two weeks later. The voyage to Pusan took almost three weeks in slow-moving cargo ships, so early excitement soon faded. Even though GIs knew they would go into combat upon landing, they still settled into listless boredom.

Ted Sprouse spent a lot of time with Sergeant Cloud. They discussed many things in general, but soldiering always in detail. Sprouse was picking Cloud's brains about combat, since the latter had been in World War II. They even talked about courage and chances of survival. "Thank God we're in artillery, not infantry," Cloud said in summation. "At least we have people between us and the enemy!"

Even though troops reacted apathetically, Sprouse led them through physical training on deck. He had to make a stab at keeping them in shape for rigorous days ahead. Almost daily he attended a briefing on the situation in Korea, where UN forces continued to fight a delaying action.

Somewhat encouraging, Americans had recovered from

21

the early disaster that had befallen Task Force Smith—the ill-prepared troops first sent into Korea from Japan—and were now fighting with determination. The objective now was to stop the enemy along the Naktong River in the west, buying time for the 2nd Infantry Division, a Marine Regiment and an Army Regimental Combat Team to get ashore at Pusan. With these reinforcements, MacArthur would be able to mount a counteroffensive.

So there was reason for optimism. In fact, flamboyant MacArthur announced the "enemy had lost his great chance for victory." Of course, the brilliant general knew all about wars and strategy—or so Sergeant Sprouse and his cohorts sailing on the high seas thought. Ironically, MacArthur lacked a critical bit of information at the time. New arrivals would proceed at peril in challenging communist forces on the land mass of Asia.

III
LAND OF SHATTERED CALM

The 38th Infantry Regiment—the Rock of the Marne commanded by Colonel George B. Peploe—landed at Pusan on August 19th, 1950. Sergeant Sprouse's unit—the 38th Field Artillery Battalion commanded by Lieutenant Colonel Robert J. O'Donnell—landed a few days later. Since the two units were to pair up in battle, they assembled together in the vicinity of Miryang.

UN forces were holding a perimeter anchored on Masan, Taegu and Kyongju. The Naktong River barred enemy from the west—but barely! The Naktong looked formidable on a map; however, it could be waded at wide spots where water was relatively shallow and flowed slowly. In fact, North Koreans had already penetrated the barrier at several points in their push to oust UN forces.

As soon as men and equipment were on hand, Captain Kasko's C Battery went to reinforce the 24th Infantry Division on the Naktong River line. This made sense because artillery is seldom in reserve and the 24th Infantry needed help. Then, too, the move enabled new arrivals to "get their feet wet." As a consequence, Sprouse's crew fired its first round in anger before the end of the month.

Eventually, the entire 2nd Infantry Division replaced the decimated 24th, so C Battery rejoined the Indianheads in time for the breakout soon to follow. Sprouse appreciated the opportunity to gain combat experience, but he was happy to return to his parent unit where he saw familiar faces all around.

The 2nd Infantry Division sector centered on a lake surrounded by swamps and rice paddies. Otherwise, low rolling hills overlooked the Naktong River. Infantry occupied hills while artillery set up in defiles behind them. Roads were inadequate for shifting or resupplying troops so engineers quickly scraped out more dry-weather roads.

There was yet another complication to fighting on the perimeter. White-clothed Korean refugees carrying belongings streamed southeasterly ahead of the advancing enemy. Thus, masses of humanity clogged roads, trails and river crossings. American GIs had neither time nor opportunity to screen refugees for infiltrators, so the enemy was able to sneak inside UN positions. Consequently, even as he fired artillery to support front-line troops, Sergeant Sprouse had to keep a wary eye on natives swirling about his position.

North Korean infiltrators frequently planted mines, set up ambushes, attacked artillery and supply sites and wiped out command posts. Worse still, they sowed suspicion concerning all Koreans! Frustrated GIs soon concluded all "gooks" should be shot on the spot. Therefore, Sprouse kept an eye on his own men to prevent their dealing with Korean civilians ruthlessly and summarily.

Touch-and-go fighting continued along the perimeter until X Corps—made up of Marines and the U.S. 7th Infantry Division—carried out MacArthur's Inchon landing on September 15th. The stroke was MacArthur's genius in full bloom and soon North Koreans were looking over their shoulders toward a threatened rear area. Now was the time for UN perimeter forces to turn the tables on their tormentors.

The Indianheads struck westward on September 23rd. The 38th Infantry Regiment, backed up by 38th Field Artillery, crossed the Naktong River and seized Ch'ogye. Sprouse's battery fired into surrounding hills of the village as infantry drove the defenders out and occupied the village. Next, the 38th Infantry joined the 23rd Infantry in an attack on Hyopchon. After losing some 300 men in short order, the

North Koreans fled. In doing so, they exposed themselves to further battering.

If there is fun in war, it's when a victorious army chases a beaten foe—especially a foe that formerly had the upper hand. UN air forces now bombed and strafed fleeing columns of enemy. Ground forces pursued relentlessly, overrunning and capturing whole units trying to escape.

Sergeant Sprouse's outfit followed closely behind the infantry. Gun crews would set up howitzers, destroy an obstacle or two, break down, charge down the road, and set up again. The hectic pace continued day and night to give the enemy no respite.

Eighth Army Commanding General Walton Walker was now in his element. An armor officer, he could apply lessons learned under General George Patton during World War II. Walker's reconnaissance and armored units followed major roads and slashed the NKPA into ribbons. It was a heady offensive for the UN while it lasted.

By September 26th, the Rock of the Marne Regiment and supporting units closed on Kochang, having advanced forty miles from the Naktong River. This was just the beginning. The spearhead drove another seventy miles westward, over the next two days to reach Chonju. It was a wild ride, indeed! Wide open flanks left Sprouse and his crew vulnerable to bands of fleeing enemy. Frequently, small arms fire came Sprouse's way as he rolled onward.

Of course, this was not an isolated drive. North Koreans were in headlong retreat all across the peninsula. On September 30th UN units crossed the 38th Parallel, invading North Korea—which introduced a whole new phase to the war.

Meanwhile, the Indianhead Division reached the Kum River above Nonsan. With its sector now pinched off, Indianheads turned to clearing out enemy pockets around

Taejon as the main attack continued northward.

Mopping up North Koreans became mainly the task of reconnaissance and infantry units, with artillery on call in an emergency. As a result, Sergeant Sprouse's outfit went into bivouac near Seoul from where it could rush in any direction on short notice. It now appeared the North Koreans would be wiped out completely in a matter of weeks. A popular rumor summed up the mood: "War over by Thanksgiving! Home by Christmas!" And the optimism was not limited to just the Korean battlefields!

When President Harry Truman met with General MacArthur at Wake Island in mid-October, the two leaders discussed handling "defeated" North Korea. Kim Il Sung had to go, of course, and all of Korea would be united under a popularly elected government. MacArthur was well qualified to deal with such diplomacy, having carried off a similar mission in Japan after World War II. If he could democratize Japanese, surely he could do the same for unsophisticated Koreans.

Almost as an afterthought, President Truman asked about the Chinese coming into the war. MacArthur's confident reply was that he doubted this would occur, but in any case modernized UN forces would handle the ill-equipped Chinese Communist Forces (CCF) readily enough. No sweat! With victory seemingly at hand, battlefield planning proceeded accordingly.

When North Korea's capital, Pyongyang, fell to the UN, logisticians quickly turned it into a supply base. Shortly, Air Force planes began landing on the Pyongyang airfield, ferrying in administrators and essentials to hasten the war's end and initiate plans for the occupation. Confidently, Eighth Army sent General Ned Almond's X Corps by landing craft to the east coast at Wonsan, positioning forces to clean out all Northeastern Korea.

UN commanders now believed they had enough men and material to finish the military campaign, so pipelines from the United States began to shut down. It must be remembered that Korea was never the main threat to United States security—that distinction belonged to Europe threatened by the Soviet Union. So the sooner Allies could put Korea behind them, the better off they would be in dealing with Joseph Stalin.

On that note, the Indianhead Division began preparing for return to general reserve in the United States. Units with heavy equipment, such as the 38th Field Artillery, were told to ready guns and vehicles for sea voyage home. At the same time, the bulk of the 2nd Infantry Division moved to Pyongyang on October 20th to guard the former North Korean capital.

With such promising prospects, Sergeant Ted Sprouse began thinking more of personal matters. With good reason, too. His son Steve was born in early September and Ted was anxious to see the baby as soon as possible. If he could rejoin his wife and visit his parents, brothers and sisters in Drakesville at Christmastime, that would be great! If not then, as soon as possible would have to do.

Sprouse and Cloud relaxed at a Bob Hope show in Seoul, the event itself being yet another indication that things were going well. Afterwards, he penned zesty notes to his wife and family. In a note to Shirley on October 26th, Ted cited his address as "Hell Hole, Korea." He asked

Sergeants Don Cloud, Ted Sprouse and Sam Chapman (and unidentified soldier) relax in Korea, 1950.

if baby Steve resembled his old man and quipped goodnaturedly that his offspring would be a good baseball player—at least an enthusiastic rooter for his dad!

What a rollercoaster Ted's two months in Korea had been. From a toehold on the Pusan Perimeter, UN forces had raced some four hundred miles northward to the approaches to the Yalu River on the Manchurian border. Now it was just a matter of time before victory would be complete, and he would leave this "hell hole." Such heady reflections only intensified the irony of what was transpiring.

An indication of trouble came when Captain Kasko told noncommissioned officers to take their 105-mm howitzers out of cosmolene—a preservative for ocean shipment—and to get ready for a trip north. The 1st Cavalry Division had run into an ambush of some sort and needed assistance. At the time it didn't appear to be anything serious; this was probably a temporary setback that would soon be turned around. Additional artillery support was the usual remedy in such cases and it usually worked.

As Sergeant Sprouse headed up the road to North Korea in early November, however, he learned that the entire 2nd Infantry Division was on the move. Perhaps it was because Eighth Army commanders wanted all the troops they could get in the final offensive to end the war. "Better to have too many than too few," Sprouse told his friend Don Cloud. So even though the abrupt change was disappointing, Sprouse still clung to the hope that he would be heading home soon. Surely the North Korean Army—so badly beaten and decimated—could not cause mischief anymore.

IV
SHIFTING BATTLEFIELDS

When the Chinese Communist Force (CCF) first attacked the U.S. 8th Cavalry near Unsan on November 1st, General MacArthur still didn't believe they had come to stay. He knew Chinese "volunteers" were south of the Yalu, but he thought they would scoot back north when hit hard. And sure enough, the Chinese faded away after skirmishing a few days.

What MacArthur didn't know, however, was that some 300,000 Chinese were closing into Korea's north-central mountains. Then, too, thousands more were on call across the Yalu River, backed up by the world's most populous nation. Indeed, the Chinese were about to deal a startling and devastating blow.

Americans miscalculated in yet another way. They still clung to World War II notions that Chinamen couldn't fight well. But under Mao Tse-tung, eager young officers of deep resolve and utter ruthlessness now led the CCF. Although Chinamen still fought with what they carried on their backs, they were patient—determined to win and willing to work and die for their cause—and they had a plan! In fact, hundreds were laboring at the time to turn a primitive cart track into a supply route between Huichon and Tokchon that would facilitate a monstrous offensive just ahead.

That first incursion against the 8th Cavalry was but one probe of UN positions by the CCF. Others were well underway at the same time against Republic of Korea Army (ROK) units, scouting for gaps and weaknesses. However, until preparations were completed, the main body of Chinese soldiers huddled in winter clothing both uncounted and discounted.

Concurrently, General Walton Walker's Eighth Army was plotting to undertake an all-out offensive to end the Korean Conflict. As part of assembling units, the 2nd Infantry Division had moved to Kunuri. From there Indianheads would advance along the Chongchon River toward Huichon, cleaning out North Korean remnants or any Chinese who happened to be in the way. Unbeknownst to the Americans, however, Huichon was the main Chinese command center and assembly area—a figurative hornets' nest, to be sure.

On November 24th, Captain Kasko's C Battery backed up the Rock of the Marne Regiment as usual. The river was on the left and ROK units were on the right. Of note, Indianheads were keeping a wary eye on the ROKs because at that stage they were not considered reliable—especially if surprised.

As for Ted Sprouse, he did not think about Chinese being in Korea. Surely, his leaders knew what they were doing. Besides, what could he do about it anyway? Ted's job was to shoot 105-mm shells on call, whatever the target. Then, too, a reassuring bit of news put UN forces near the Yalu River on several fronts. Maybe the fighting would end soon.

Naturally, Ted and his comrades wanted this war ended as soon as possible. Temperatures hovered near zero, freezing hydraulic systems and making engines hard to start. Radios would not work because batteries failed and weapons would not always function reliably. Cold weather made a mess of everything else as well. Rations and drinking water froze solid and troops found it impossible to keep warm. The Army still didn't have adequate arctic gear, so GIs had to get by with clothing designed for warmer climates. Many discarded the cold steel helmet in favor of the pile-lined cap; keeping warm seemed more important than being protected.

So Sprouse and his comrades attacked eagerly, advancing steadily against sporadic resistance. In fact, Indianheads patrolled beyond Kujang-dong without a hitch. Just about everyone was encouraged by this initial success.

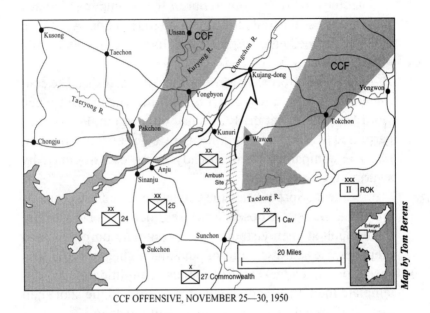

CCF OFFENSIVE, NOVEMBER 25—30, 1950

Chinese leaders also were encouraged—for quite another reason! The farther the Americans progressed, the more they opened themselves up for a crushing counterattack. Chinese patrols began working their way south to raid UN stockpiles, disrupt communications and block supply routes. Then the CCF went all out!

The Chinese main thrust after dark on November 25th split a seam between ROK regiments. To add confusion, the Chinese sounded bugles and shepherd's pipes, shook rattles and ignited fireworks. Surprised and intimidated by the on-

31

slaught and enemy raiders behind them, ROKs scrambled southward. The Chinese pursued with a vengeance and soon seized Tokchon, from where they wheeled westward to cut off Americans to the north. Straggling ROKs reassembled at Pukchong-ni, but they were out of the battle.

Chinese soldiers poured out of the mountains to attack Indianheads strung out along the road to Huichon. A stunned Colonel Peploe began turning his units to face the enemy on his right flank.

When he informed superiors, they at first insisted he continue to attack in a test of wills with the enemy. But when word trickled in that the ROKs had bugged out, Peploe was permitted to reorient his regiment toward Tokchon. However, his rifle companies were already being overwhelmed by swarming Chinese.

Sergeant Sprouse saw the Chinese overrun K Company, leaving C Battery exposed. Sprouse ordered his crew to fire point blank at enemy soldiers attacking with burp guns and grenades. He heard screams of pain that night as the 105-mm shells tore into attackers. But Sprouse had little time to contemplate the horror and agony of war; instead, he shot shell after shell in a desperate attempt to halt the enemy.

Nine K Company survivors straggled up to Sprouse's gun position. He arranged them around his gun to fend off attackers. When Captain Kasko ordered Sprouse to displace, he loaded the infantrymen on his deuce and a half. A few miles back, they set up to fight once more.

Quite unexpectedly, the Chinese went under cover at daybreak. Sprouse concluded they wanted to avoid UN air strikes. Whatever, he welcomed the break so that his crew could regroup and prepare for the next assault sure to come at nightfall.

Captain Kasko moved C Battery rearward to more defensible positions during the day. Sprouse's crewmen located the howitzer well enough, but they didn't have explosives to blast holes in the frozen ground for protection. With little choice, C Battery decided to take the Chinese under fire at first sighting, make them pay dearly for every yard of advance, and then displace rearward at the last instant. Sherman tanks eventually joined this cat-and-mouse game, adding their .50-caliber machine guns to the desperate effort of holding off the Chinese.

Sprouse's crew fought and fell back all the way to Kunuri, starting point of the offensive five days earlier. Kunuri now had to be held to keep escape routes open for troops still to the north. Of course, the Chinese wanted Kunuri in order to cut the escape routes and demolish units trying to get out. Consequently, the night of November 28th saw the fiercest fighting yet. Sprouse's men fired so many shells without letup that the gun tube overheated. A five-gallon can of ice-cold water poured down the barrel evaporated on its way to the breech. Tank-mounted machine guns also burned out from sustained firing as well. One small benefit, though: Hot gun barrels warmed shivering gun crews!

At dawn the Chinese were still short of Kunuri. Sprouse looked out over the battlefield to see dead scattered across a bleak landscape. "How long can this go on?" he wondered.

Others pondered the course of the war as well. Eighth Army Commander General Walker concluded he was in desperate straits. Clearly, it would take months to mount another offensive. Prudently, he recommended withdrawing his forces far enough south to establish a solid defense; his recommendation was reinforced from elsewhere.

American X Corps under General Ned Almond in northeast Korea also had been hard hit by the Chinese and the weather. By "attacking to the rear," 1st Marine and 7th Infantry divisions narrowly escaped entrapment at "Frozen Chosin" reservoir.

General MacArthur now became cleareyed about Chinese intervention and the quality of communist soldiers. His changed perspective was reflected in a statement released by General Walker on November 29th: "That assault launched by the Eighth Army five days ago probably saved our forces from a trap which might well have destroyed them. . . . The timing of our attack to develop the situation was, indeed, fortunate." Be that as it may, General Walker ordered UN forces southward as far as Pyongyang.

Taking advantage of mobility and air cover, Eighth Army units lost little time pulling back. The 2nd Infantry Division, protecting the UN flank at Kunuri, would stay until November 30th. Then, the 9th Infantry Regiment would lead the withdrawal, followed by the 38th Infantry and assorted units interspersed throughout the column. The 23rd Infantry, under Colonel Paul Freeman, would fend off the enemy and leave last.

But again the Chinese were a step ahead. Instead of letting UN forces slip away, the CCF infiltrated southward—even as night gave way to day! Apparently this opportunity was worth the risk of exposure to UN air strikes.

GIs, lulled into believing they had another daytime reprieve, did not heed disturbing signs even when they saw them. Perhaps they felt secure in the midst of all the firepower assembled at Kunuri. An impressive sight it was, too. Three artillery battalions with eighteen guns each and Sherman tanks with machine guns and high velocity 76-mm guns. Then, too, infantrymen were marching southward to clear out a roadblock on the road to Sunchon.

Out of habit, Sprouse and Cloud got together, talking, smoking, and drinking coffee. Both relaxed, knowing they would soon head south and into a less hostile environment. Until now, they had been forced to fight on the enemy's terms, but once out of the mountains odds would shift as air power and fire power came into play.

"Look out there," Cloud said as he pointed southward. In early daylight, several Chinese in white clothing were walking southward along the railroad tracks. They were carrying weapons and back packs and seemed in no particular hurry. Nor did Americans all around seem particularly concerned.

"Where do you suppose they're going?" Sprouse asked his friend.

"I don't know," was the reply. "But they're not coming at us."

Maybe if Sprouse and Cloud—and all the others—had not been so tired and cold they would have been more perceptive. Perhaps they would have suspected that what enemy they saw was only the tip of a very large iceberg. But after pressure-filled days it was indeed a relief to see enemy soldiers walking away.

A glance at Map 2 will show that two routes led to Sunchon—and out of entrapment. Major General Laurence B. ("Dutch") Keiser chose the most direct way in order to avoid competing with the 25th Infantry Division to the west for crowded road space. However, Keiser did send his supply trains west to Anju. As for the combat units, he would lead them straight south to Sunchon.

Although Chinese infiltrators had already blocked the intended route, General Keiser was confident his 9th Infantry would brush them aside and crash on through. Earlier in the day a truck convoy from Sunchon had made it, although it had been fired on twice. Encouraging, too, was news that the British Commonwealth Brigade was attacking northward from Sunchon, thereby shortening the Indianheads' escape route.

Taking advantage of daylight, the division reconnaissance company and a platoon of tanks started south at noon. When the CCF did not interfere, other elements charged onto the road. General Keiser near the head of the column noted a few incoming rifle shots and a couple mortar rounds, but he had expected as much. The withdrawal was on track at that point.

Just before the Taedong River, however, the road channelized through a quarter-mile-long cut in a hill with steep banks on both sides. When vehicles loaded with GIs entered this choke point, the Chinese opened fire with small arms and 82-mm mortars. Then sappers scurried down hillsides and tossed satchel charges onto trucks and huddling troops. Vehicles jammed into one another and shut down traffic pushing in from the north. The Indianhead Division was being caught up in a daylight ambush extending miles.

Scarcely able to believe such enemy "foolhardiness," the Air Force responded. P-51 Mustangs strafed, napalmed, and bombed to a fare-thee-well—whenever and wherever they spotted an enemy target. But the Chinese gutted out brief, furious strikes from the sky—and kept right on punishing entrapped ground troops.

When daylight began to fade in the mountains, Mustangs suspended operations and returned to air bases. There, over hot food and a drink or two, pilots exchanged war stories. Perhaps some even felt pity for the hapless Chinese they had strafed and bombed so brutally.

But Indianheads on the ground—the Ted Sprouses— were left to deal with reality. And reality was not pretty! At the outset, many had vaulted from trucks in a dash to cover, dissolving combat units. Thus, commanders lost control of riflemen who could have dealt with ambushers. What had started as an orderly withdrawal turned into a chaotic every-man-for-himself attempt to escape.

Waiting in late afternoon with the last unit to join the long column, Sergeant Sprouse and his comrades were unaware of the grim confusion up ahead. They heard shooting, of course, and saw P-51s swooping in, but waiting GIs assumed the planes were demolishing a reported two-mile roadblock on the road to Sunchon.

Sprouse was greatly relieved when ordered to hit the road. Cloud's truck led, followed by Sprouse's and then Sam Chapman's. Sprouse had eight other men on board. Corporal Don Roe was driving with Sprouse in the cab beside him. One soldier manned the ring-mounted .50-caliber machine gun over the cab. Others sat scanning the hills in gathering darkness. All were nervous as they listened to sounds of battle up ahead.

The convoy moved along steadily for a few miles, where the road was open and straight. When lead vehicles entered the open end of a giant horseshoe of mountains, however, the narrow road twisted and steepened drastically. To negotiate turns, Roe had to back and advance several times. Then Captain Kasko radioed a stark message: "Look out for enemy over the next twelve miles!"

While Sprouse was still absorbing the import of the captain's message, Cloud's truck pulled to a halt. When Cloud got out of the cab, Roe and Sprouse joined him. Ahead they heard shooting and explosions, which seemed to be coming closer. This was serious!

"Sarge, here they come at us!" Roe shouted as he pointed to the left.

Sure enough! In light of a full moon, Sprouse picked up shadows maneuvering on the hillside above. He pointed out the enemy and ordered the machine gunner to open fire. Others joined in with rifles as well. Chinese burp guns retaliated and an incoming mortar round dropped nearby. The roadway ahead was blocked with enemy swarming all around!

Reflexively, GIs unhooked howitzers and readied to fire point blank. Sprouse started with "Willie Peter," white phosphorous shells that not only burned and shocked Chinese soldiers but lit up hillside shadows as well.

The loader shouted "Up!" and the gunner pulled the lanyard. Surprise! Not only did the projectile dart forward, but the howitzer recoiled clean off the road! Gun trails would not "dig" into the frozen road bed. The crew wrestled the heavy gun back onto the road and set up once more. Upon firing, the gun again jumped backward, so repositioning had to be repeated. Still, the effort was effective.

The exploding white phosphorous shells stunned the Chinese momentarily, seemed to confuse them. When the enemy stopped firing, Sprouse switched to high explosive shells in order to further discourage ambushers.

"We got 'em on the run!" Roe cheered from atop the truck.

Captain Kasko walked up at that point and said, "Good work, men." After cautioning them to stay alert, the captain departed—never to return!

Unfortunately, this band of fighting artillerymen was the exception that perilous night. Too many others had scampered away, leaving a few stalwart pockets to fight off the CCF. Despairing, Sprouse concluded that unless someone rallied GIs for a united defense, all would be lost. But his pleas and calls for help to panicky soldiers passing by were ignored or spurned.

"Here they come again!" Roe announced from his lookout post.

Scarcely had the words left Roe's mouth when an incoming 82-mm mortar round dropped nearby. A deafening explosion hurled fragments and debris into vehicles, equipment and humans alike. Roe was the most seriously injured of all.

Sergeant Cloud rushed up to where Sprouse was attempting to remove an eight-inch steel shard embedded in Roe's right thigh. Cloud tried as well but to no avail. The blood-slickened fragment was stuck fast in flesh and bone. Sprouse made a tourniquet with Roe's belt and stopped most of the bleeding. They lifted Roe into the deuce and a half, and told him to loosen the tourniquet every ten minutes.

Bludgeoned by American artillery, the Chinese decided to respond in kind. Mortar round after mortar round now plummeted onto the trapped GIs. Sporadically, burp guns raked the stalled column as well. The Chinese were methodically destroying everyone and everything.

All three C Battery gun sections now focused on enemy mortars, zeroing in on propellant flashes on the hillside. Apparently, the CCF had not dug in the weapons, for artillery silenced several. Sprouse believed they could hold out as long as artillery ammunition was at hand, but what then?

Sprouse momentarily lost his nerve. He noted others kneeling and praying, so he dropped to his knees in a ditch beside the road and for the first time really prayed!

"Dear God," he pleaded, "if you'll get me back to my wife and son, I'll do all I can for you the rest of my life."

It wasn't much of a prayer, but Sprouse felt better for having made the bid. Very shortly—and for months on end—Ted Sprouse was to ponder the quirks of Divine intervention.

Ted called remnants of C Battery together. The immediate question was whether to leave now or to gut it out till dawn when UN aircraft took to the skies again. Or perhaps a friendly counterattack might drive off the Chinese ambushers. Even at that stage, Ted Sprouse wasn't willing to believe UN forces would leave the battlefield in such disarray.

The meeting was cut short by an incoming mortar round that hit the group dead center. Sprouse shook himself out of a daze as he lay upon the ground. Feeling pain in his right leg, he touched the area and his hand came away sticky—blood! Then he noted his right hand had also been lacerated. He fumbled with his first aid packet until the bandage opened.

"I hope I can walk," he muttered as he applied the bandage to his leg. The hand would have to stay uncovered.

Others around him were worse off—by far! No one was moving. All appeared to be dead. Two men nearby had no faces anymore, disfigured beyond recognition! Was he the lone survivor of those so intent on escaping just a moment ago? And, if so, why him?

"Hey Cloud!" he shouted in near panic. "You all right?"

Don Cloud rushed up, relieved to see his friend had survived. He checked out Sprouse's leg and concluded he "wasn't hurt too bad." Reassured, Sprouse got to his feet and joined Cloud in checking out the others. Together, they loaded dead and wounded on the deuce and a half. Although it made little sense under the circumstances, they felt getting *their* men off the cold ground was the humane thing to do.

With Chinese creeping near, C Battery remnants returned to their guns. Since most of those killed and wounded were from Chapman's crew, Sprouse and Cloud sent men to operate Chapman's howitzer. They managed to hold the CCF at bay until ammunition ran out at midnight, which ended all hope of holding out till daylight. They had to get away now— or never!

Sergeant Chapman was in bad shape. "My ulcers are bleeding," he confided to Sprouse. "You and Cloud have to do it from here on. I'll tag along as long as I can."

Sprouse and Cloud redistributed ammunition and grenades so everyone was armed. They made a stretcher for Roe.

40

Lastly, they destroyed howitzers by dropping thermite grenades down tubes.

Altogether nineteen men slipped away from the ambush site in early hours of December 1st. All were wounded, all were sickened, all were dead tired. Yet they took turns, four at a time, carrying Roe.

Relying on his native-American instincts, Sergeant Don Cloud led the way. He started southward but kept bumping into Chinese patrols or gunfire. Since they had been at the end of the road column, Cloud now concluded the quickest way out of encirclement was to head north. Also, the Chinese would not be expecting such a move. Once clear of the ambush site, Cloud intended to turn westward toward Anju. If lucky, they might run into other Eighth Army troops still retreating toward Sunchon.

The drawback, of course, was the added distance: Now they would have to traverse about fifteen miles over mountains in darkness just to reach the other road. Yet, they had no choice but to push on while it was still dark.

Even though blood trickled down his leg to collect in his boot, Sprouse tried to ignore his wound. He took his turn carrying Roe, despite unsteadiness in walking. The initial surge of adrenaline upon leaving the ambush site soon wore off and discouragement set in. Then, of course, they had doubled back; consequently, Ted concluded they had gone only a couple miles when they took their first break.

Sprouse sat on a rock and pressed the bandage against his wound to stop bleeding. A chill quickly engulfed him. It all seemed so futile. He was tempted to lie down, fall asleep and just freeze to death. He had heard that was an easy way to die.

As he was about to give in, the thought struck him: Time was critical! They had to distance themselves from the enemy before dawn! They had to speed things up somehow.

Roe! They had to do something about Roe; carrying him was ruining their chances of getting away. Sprouse got up and found Cloud, proposed a solution.

"I don't know if Roe'll buy that," Cloud mused.

"Let me talk to him," Sprouse countered. "I'll reason with him."

Sprouse explained to Roe that they would hide him in a cave, leave food, water and bullets. "That's the only way we can make it," Sprouse concluded. "But don't worry, I'll personally lead rescuers back to get you out as soon as we reach friendly lines." He had never been more sincere in his whole life.

But Roe wouldn't hear of it. "Don't leave me up here," he pleaded. "Just get me on my feet and I'll make it. Swear to God I will!"

"The Chinese are all around us," Sprouse argued. "You even moan and we're all goners."

"You won't hear a peep outa me," Roe said as he struggled up from the stretcher.

With Sprouse's help, Roe took one gingerly step, then another. How could his grittiness be ignored? So with Roe clutching Sprouse's arm, they followed Cloud up the mountain path. Others fell in line, picking their way over the rugged terrain. For a while, they moved faster, every step carrying them away from the ghostly ambush site.

As might be expected, the Chinese hurried to exploit their smashing victory. They pursued retreating Americans on all fronts, crowding them ever southward—further isolating those left behind. And the CCF sent combat patrols sweeping across all escape routes, relentlessly tracking down would-be escapees.

Twice that night Sprouse's band bumped into enemy patrols and twice managed to get away after an exchange of hand grenades. Cloud paused at daybreak to rest and plan anew. Sprouse joined him in a hollowed-out spot, but there was to be no respite.

"Have another grenade?" Cloud whispered.

"A couple," Sprouse answered.

"Over there," Cloud said as he pointed.

Sprouse hurled the grenade to the indicated spot. The Chinese hurled one back! So Sprouse hurled another in retaliation—the last thing he would recall. When he came to, his mouth was covered by Cloud's hand.

"Be quiet!" Cloud admonished.

"What happened?"

"A concussion grenade knocked you out," Cloud explained. "Lucky you're not dead."

Sprouse now was pretty sure "someone up there" was looking out for him. His lower back throbbed, but his leg no longer hurt. Instead, the limb felt numb; however, he could move it well enough. He would be able to walk. Miraculously, Cloud had escaped injury altogether. Sprouse repeated his vow to serve God during what remained of his life.

They decided to lie low until nightfall. With ammunition nearly depleted, they couldn't risk another firefight in broad daylight. The nineteen Americans scattered into bushes and among rocks, or lay in natural depressions where they covered themselves with twigs, leaves, even snow. Throughout the day, Chinese soldiers passed near but didn't discover anyone. Obviously, they knew GIs were in the vicinity. As he shivered throughout the day, Sprouse thanked God for short winter days and long winter nights.

At dusk they gathered and set out once more. It felt good to be up and moving. Cloud led northward, picking his way along paths the others could follow. Sprouse kept telling himself the worst was over. They had gotten away, hadn't they? Surely, it was just a matter of time and distance before they escaped encirclement, before they bumped into friendly troops.

Of course, Sprouse had no idea how far they would have to go. The UN would probably set up defenses near Pyongyang, some thirty miles south of Sunchon. But because of twists and turns, the escape route would be much longer than following roads. Nonetheless, Sprouse remained hopeful.

They climbed a ridgeline leading to the top of an imposing hill southwest of Kunuri. They reached the crest without incident; however, Cloud said he was sure they were being followed. Two other ridgelines led downward. Cloud chose the one leading westward, but as he neared the valley below he heard the Chinese talking. The Americans retraced their steps and took the third ridge northward. Again Chinese soldiers were heard talking below. Obviously, they had surrounded the Americans.

In deep despair, the nineteen GIs struggled back up the hill. Sprouse and Cloud set up a ring of security while they tried to figure a way out. Sprouse saw one possibility—and a slim one it was.

Supposing the two of them stole away, leaving the others to fend for themselves. Would not the Chinese assume they had captured everyone when they eventually overran the hilltop? Sprouse and Cloud would hide in mining caves found throughout North Korea. After a week or so they would begin working their way southward through a less vigilant enemy. They even rationalized they would lead rescuers back—somehow! —to free the others. Cloud listened closely, even added a suggestion or two.

Ultimately, they abandoned the desperate scheme. As

44

Sprouse reminded Cloud, "If we desert guys who trust us, I don't believe I can live with myself." So it came down to

Indianhead artillery pieces and vehicles destroyed in the ambush below Kunuri.

being loyal to their followers. All nineteen would escape or be captured together.

Suspense did not last long. As the second day of December dawned clear and cold, the Chinese closed in. Sprouse and Cloud watched helplessly as GIs were rooted out around them. One here, two there. And so on. Finally, it was Cloud and Sprouse's turn.

As Sprouse watched enemy soldiers awkwardly approach, he thought of those walking down the railroad tracks south of Kunuri three days earlier. Sprouse knew now where the Chinese had been heading—and why! Of course, Cloud now also knew—as did the other 3,000 Indianheads who did not make it through the ambush that fateful day and night.

The 2nd Infantry Division artillery lost nearly half its men. The 38th Field Artillery Battalion was hardest hit, losing its eighteen 105-mm howitzers and all its vehicles. Its commander, Lieutenant Colonel Robert O'Donnel, was wounded five times but survived and was awarded the Silver Star for his valiant attempts to hold his unit together.

But there had been another way. When Colonel Freeman's 23rd Infantry departed Kunuri the last day of November, men and vehicles headed due west to Anju rather than south to Sunchon. At Anju, the column turned left and passed by Sunchon unscathed. Actually, Colonel Freeman had little choice at the time—the Kunuri-Sunchon road was blocked from end to end.

Although losses on the ill-chosen road were high, the toll did not end when escaping remnants of the 2nd Infantry Division struggled through Sunchon. For those lost as prisoners of war, the battle had shifted to other fields. Indeed, their ordeal had just begun.

V
A TWISTING MARCH

Ted Sprouse was incredulous when an enemy's bayonet prodded him to his feet. A Chinese captor jerked away Sprouse's weapon and shoved him toward others being gathered up. Ted raised his hands above his head in abject surrender—he was a prisoner of war! Never had he felt so humiliated.

Still Sprouse hadn't given up entirely. He had concealed a .45 caliber pistol with three rounds in the clip under his overcoat. Insufficient now against some twenty enemy swarming about, the three rounds would suffice when the number of guards dropped to two or three. Then Sprouse would whip out the pistol, shoot the guards, and he and eighteen others would escape. For the time being, however, Sprouse had to be patient—and retain the pistol.

Even as the Chinese collected prisoners, UN fighter-bombers dived in to strafe and bomb the hilltop for an hour or so—pilots not realizing they were punishing Americans as well as Chinese. Still, no one was injured and Sprouse was grateful pilot accuracy was not as good as often claimed.

Ordnance expended, the planes winged homeward, leaving hapless prisoners to ponder ironies of warfare. Supposing the airstrike had come sooner? Or supposing bullets and bombs had been both selective and effective against the enemy? So near, yet so far, freedom!

Captors lost little time in herding captives into a huge cave halfway down the hill. In the nick of time, too, for bombers now appeared and pummeled a village at the foot of the hill. When bombs exploded, dirt and rocks dropped from the ceiling on those huddled below. Paradoxically, guards seemed less concerned about being bombed than did their prisoners.

47

Communists had confidence in their doctrine of passive air defense. How significant were episodes of shaking ground, loud noises and whistling bombs in the context of a global test of wills that would go on until one side or the other won? Marx said history was on the side of communists, so why worry? More practical considerations now took over, as Chinese guards began taking dog tags, rings, watches, money, cigarettes, food and clothing from prisoners in the dimly lit cavern.

Sprouse nervously waited out his turn, wondering whether he might lose the pistol—and his last chance of escape. He was relieved when a senior guard interrupted the search with hurried instructions, after which prisoners were rushed out of the cave.

Air raids had ended, so prisoners were marched back up the hill. There they sat with hands above their heads in the midst of a circle of guards. Machine guns were in place, reminiscent of a scenario Sprouse had witnessed once before in South Korea. In that instance, UN prisoners lay dead with arms and feet bound by their own shoestrings. Was such a calculated massacre to be his fate now?

In lowered voices, Cloud and Sprouse discussed what they would do. They agreed to tumble over at the first burst of machine-gun fire and play dead. Perhaps a non-fatal wound would add realism. Afterwards, the Chinese would surely move on, assuming all prisoners were dead. How they would manage after that—assuming everything went as planned—never came to mind; Sprouse and Cloud only sought to survive the moment.

Hour after hour passed with the guards seemingly unsure of their next step. Apparently, they were following instructions, because at midnight the machine guns were picked up and carried away and prisoners ordered to their feet. Standing up was almost impossible after having sat so long in near-zero temperatures. To regain circulation, Sprouse stamped the ground as he walked.

Guards hustled them down the hill to the village bombed earlier in the day. There a communist leader explained in broken English what was to happen. Prisoners strained to glean something useful, something encouraging, something enlightening. However, a rambling discourse sprinkled with communist jargon—"peace-loving Koreans," "warmongering capitalists," and "freedom-loving Chinese volunteers"—only served to confuse and frustrate captives. Of course, this was but a small dose of what prisoners would experience in days ahead.

More to the point, Chinese guards passed among prisoners to remove any jewelry or useful items that may have been overlooked in the cave. A young GI in front of Sprouse had difficulty removing his wedding band, so the guard whacked off the swollen finger with a knife. Sprouse resisted an urge to protest, lest guards focus on him and find the pistol. But he knew now he would kill these "animals" when the opportunity came.

No mention of food, rest, water or destination, of course. Humane treatment was not in the cards for captured Americans. Forget the Geneva Conventions! Prisoners began to realize that henceforth there would be no rules, no mercy in this psychological game that was as ruthless as it was novel.

Spouse welcomed the march that began that night. Even though tired and suffering pain, he mustered surprising energy. Anything was preferable to sitting, standing hours at a time with nothing to do but think. Surely, somewhere ahead there would be a prison camp that would offer some semblance of normality, stability, even security. So every step taken now was a bit of progress, wasn't it?

For twelve nights they marched—in circles! During daylight they rested in caves, shelters, huts or under cover that hid them from the air. Sprouse was confused at the outset, especially when they passed the ambush site on the Kunuri-Sunchon road night after night. Then it dawned on him that they were being mentally tortured. But for what purpose?

No food at all in the first four days. By then hunger pangs were subsiding and many had resigned themselves to never eating again. Subsisting only on water dipped from streams or melted from snow, prisoners were wasting away fast. Perhaps this was to be their fate—they would starve to death. Sprouse recalled pictures of captured American soldiers on the Bataan death march in World War II. All were gaunt looking, half starved. Of course, the weather there had been hot; in Korea it was beastly cold, perhaps the worst of the two extremes.

Then, at the end of a day in a mud hut with barely room to stand, each prisoner was given a handful of field corn softened by boiling water. That was it! Still, most consumed the meager rations; it was a diet they would grow accustomed to—even look forward to—during this twisting march. Every tasteless kernel would help survive another day.

On one of the stops at the ambush site, Sprouse spotted his deuce and a half nearby. Everything was as they had left it *that* night. Corpses, amazingly preserved in the cold weather, were strewn about. Closer examination revealed gnawings by predatory animals, however.

Sprouse recalled some C-rations lying around in the bed of his truck, mostly undesirable choices in former days. Now even a can of hash that he had always loathed seemed appealing. But when he peered into the bedbox he couldn't see a single can remaining—all had been carried off by Korean scavengers.

After an overnight stay in a large vacant schoolhouse,

Chinese guards ordered prisoners to remove outer clothing for a thorough search. The pistol would now be found! Sprouse had not been able to carry out his "ambush" because there were always more guards present than he had bullets.

Then, too, he had grown less sanguine over prospects of carrying out the scheme as time went on. Even if he had been able to shoot the guards and get away, prisoners were too weakened to survive in the cold and without any food at all. Tellingly, the possibility that he might be shot for concealing the weapon did not alarm him now.

However, Cloud was more concerned and more imaginative. "Slip me the gun," he whispered. "The reds won't shoot me because I'm a Cherokee Indian. We're 'peasants' back home, you know."

"Not a chance," Sprouse replied. "It's been my plot all along and I'll take the consequences. Besides, I'm not sure I'll make it anyway."

"Don't talk that way, Ted," Cloud rasped under his breath. "We'll both make it or neither of us will! So, snap out of it!"

Sprouse was embarrassed by his own momentary loss of resolve—and impressed by Cloud's display of selflessness. No doubt about it, Cloud was about the best friend a man could ever have. Well, Sprouse, too, would give it a hell of a go!

Thus fortified, he calmly awaited his fate.

The pistol was found as expected, but the guard seemed puzzled. Then he was humbled by a superior for not having discovered the weapon previously. Next, all guards took a lacing for their laxity. Lost in the furor was the fact that Sprouse had attempted to conceal a weapon, a serious infraction indeed. The upshot was that Sprouse got away cleanly, except that he had lost his best hope for getting away.

Corporal Don Roe continued to inspire everyone as the

days passed. The gritty guy hobbled along with the shell fragment still embedded in his thigh, the wound oozing pus and blood. Fearing a trigger-happy guard might decide to put Roe out of his misery with a shot to the head, Sprouse examined his friend's wound during a marching halt.

Putrid flesh had loosened around the shard, so Ted decided to "operate." He put his arms around Roe and held him tightly while Cloud and another GI jerked the fragment free. Afterwards, Roe's thigh looked ghastly and smelled horribly but the "surgery" seemed successful.

Roe was elated and said he felt "a hell of a lot better." Sprouse was concerned the infection would now spread and kill Roe. Nonetheless, Ted "bandaged" the open wound with a piece of newspaper since there was nothing else. All first aid packets had long since been used.

Sprouse's own wound alternated between improving and worsening as the days wore on with no medical treatment. He concluded his mood had much to do with his medical evaluation, which was undoubtedly true. One thing, though, Sprouse unfailingly encouraged healing by removing the bandage and airing it in sunlight. He also exposed the wound to the sun's rays on warmer days. Afterwards, he would replace the soiled bandage, hoping primitive sterilization would work.

Odors were not noticeable while prisoners were in open air, but inside cramped quarters body stench became unbearable. No one had bathed since capture and even rudimentary sanitation was out of the question. Still, Sprouse "washed" his hands in snow before eating whenever he could. A futile gesture, perhaps, but it was the only civilized ritual remaining.

On the thirteenth day, the march began to make sense. For the first time, they did not pass the ambush site; they actually entered new territory! Then, too, others began joining the formation as the reds gathered captives for the next phase. Perhaps they were finally en route to a permanent camp, which couldn't be all that far since they had started deep within North Korea.

Disturbing news a couple days later. Sergeant Sam Chapman confided his ulcers were bleeding, due to the boiled-corn diet. He didn't know how much longer he could keep up. "I should have let them evacuate me for ulcers a month ago," he said ruefully. "But I turned Doc down so that I could go home with all you guys. Now I'll never make it."

With help and assurances from Sprouse and Cloud, Chapman gamely tried to carry on. But hemorrhaging continued unabated. On the nineteenth day of the march, Sprouse helped Chapman to an outside latrine in bitter cold. Not able to squat, Chapman soiled himself thoroughly. Sprouse did his best to wash his comrade's trousers with snow as Chapman tottered half naked in freezing temperature. Back inside the shelter, Sprouse used his own overcoat in an attempt to coax warmth back into Chapman's shivering body, but to no avail. Within an hour he was dead.

Grudgingly, guards permitted a burial. Cloud, Sprouse and a couple other prisoners carried the body a short distance away and placed it in a natural depression. Without a shovel, they covered Sam Chapman's remains with snow, twigs and grass. When Sprouse paused to pray, the guard hustled them back to the shelter. On the way, Sprouse silently beseeched God to "take care of Sergeant Chapman now and forever. Amen."

Sprouse himself felt his own strength ebbing by the day. His legs and back hurt all the time, especially when he marched over uneven roads and paths. He became obsessed with the thought he would soon join Chapman in death. But Cloud was unwavering in his insistence that they would go home together—some day! More important, though, was the example Cloud set day after day by resolutely plodding along.

As the steadily growing number of prisoners struggled over a darkened mountain on Christmas eve, Ted Sprouse was treated to Divine phenomena. Just as they reached the crest at midnight, the sky turned brilliantly clear. "I had never seen a sight quite like that," he recalls. "Nor have I seen one since. But it didn't last long. Someone up there turned it off." Whether real or imagined, the event was nonetheless reassuring to Sergeant Ted Sprouse on that lonely, miserable holiday night.

As he marched along, Sprouse's thoughts turned to his wife and family. "Steve's first Christmas," he muttered under his breath, "and I've missed it." Would he ever see his wife again? Would he ever see his son at all? How was his mother holding up? Poor Ida May! He wondered if they had received official notification.

WESTERN UNION

W. P. MARSHALL, PRESIDENT

1201

1950 DEC 19

The filing time shown in the date line on telegrams and day letters is STANDARD TIME at point of origin. Time of receipt is STANDARD TIME at point of destination

MB047

M.WA304 GOVT PD=FAX WASHINGTON DC 19 153P=

MRS JOANNE S SPROUSE.

REPORT DELIVERY=ROUTE 2 CENTERVILLE IOWA=

THE SECRETARY OF THE ARMY HAS ASKED ME TO EXPRESS HIS DEEP REGRET THAT YOUR HUSBAND SGT SPROUSE TEDDY R HAS BEEN MISSING IN ACTION IN KOREA SINCE 30 NOV 50 UPON RECEIPT OF FURTHER INFORMATION IN THEIR OFFICE YOU WILL BE ADVISED IMMEDIATELY PD CONFIRMING LETTER FOLLOWS=

EDWARD F WITSELL MAJOR GENERAL USA THE ADJUTANT
GENERAL OF THE ARMY=

THE COMPANY WILL APPRECIATE SUGGESTIONS FROM ITS PATRONS CONCERNING ITS SERVICE

Official notification of Sprouse's MIA status, December 1950

Sprouse had no way of knowing, of course, but his wife had received a telegram on December 19th informing her that Ted had been missing in action since November 30th, 1950. It would be another year, however, before she would hear anything more.

Prisoners again hid in a building upon daybreak that Christmas; however, this time they found the building was "occupied." When Sprouse felt something crawling in his beard, he picked off a louse as "big as a house fly." By then everyone else was finding "companions." It was to be a losing battle; except when prisoners were outside in extreme cold, lice would roam prisoners' bodies at will.

Depression, too, became a constant companion. Many were so weak from dysentery they couldn't look after themselves. Of course, hardly anyone was up to helping anyone else. Overwhelmed, GIs drifted away to lie in the snow and freeze to death.

Demoralized prisoners sometimes lashed out in frustration over their plight. Once Sprouse heard a violent but shortlived commotion outside his shelter. Later, a bedraggled prisoner was found dead in the snow. He had been tossed outside because he had soiled himself uncontrollably. At that stage, Sprouse was ready to conclude that Americans were really no better than the "animals" guarding them. Then it dawned on him that this was what the Chinese had in mind all along. Well, there had to be a way of retaining one's sense of right and wrong, even in the hell of communist captivity.

Ted Sprouse sought consolation in friends such as Cloud and Roe. The trio stimulated each other through encouragements, scoldings, morbid jokes and helping hands. They kidded about each other's filth and gauntness. Cloud, who had no beard, was teased for not shaving. He would smirk and rejoin that being an American Indian was not all bad, now was it? Cloud's "going through this thing together" was re-peated day after day, voiced aloud to shore up his own re-solve as much as anything. And everyone needed shoring up for just when they thought the weather couldn't get any worse, they entered Death Valley.

Closed in by mountains, even sunny days in Death Val-ley lasted a mere four hours. Most days the temperature hov-ered at minus twenty-five degrees, but once it dipped to fifty-five degrees below zero! During the four days of traversing the valley, some prisoners wandered off to freeze and end it all. Guards inadvertently assisted the despairing by summarily shooting stragglers. So an occasional rifle shot reminded all that "escape" was but a trigger squeeze away.

Dietary deficiency was a continuing concern. To supple-ment the daily handful of boiled corn, Sprouse and Cloud ate frozen pumpkin rinds found at roadside. Once they found a sweet potato to share—a real treat! During a pause to relieve themselves, Cloud spotted tobacco plants and plucked dried-up leaves. Later, he and Sprouse wrapped the weed in news-print and enjoyed a smoke.

It was not possible to determine how far they had ad-vanced toward their goal, nor how far they still had to go. Sprouse guessed they marched twenty to thirty miles a night, so he would take twenty-five as an average and multiply the figure against the number of days on the road. Thus, from mid-December to mid-January they probably covered eight hundred miles, almost twice the distance from Pusan to the Yalu River! As for a destination, anytime they stayed at a spot more than a day they believed they had arrived—they were there! Inevitably, they again found themselves march-ing onward.

A change did occur, however. Once they had ventured beyond the optimum range of UN aircraft, guards switched to daytime travel. The first daylight march was delayed when guards thought a prisoner had escaped. (With so many dying and falling by the wayside, Sprouse wondered how guards could tell who was absent.) After prisoners stood at attention till noon, guards ordered the march to begin. By then prisoners' feet were frozen and benumbed. Cloud and Sprouse, helping each other, managed to stay upright as they walked, but some did not.

Occasionally, Sprouse saw a prisoner stumble, fall and lay still as others shuffled by. Although inured to the sight of death by then, Ted would still react when someone close faltered. During one halt he saw telltale signs in a man he had known since playing baseball back at Fort Lewis. Sprouse urged him to continue, even tugged the GI's arm. But the guy was a "goner," pleading, "Leave me alone, Sarge. I can't make it." Sprouse took note of the dying man's appearance: resigned, relaxed and peaceful.

When Sprouse removed his boots that night, he had no feeling in his feet. He massaged them until sensation eventually returned, but they ached and throbbed all night through. The next morning, he could not pull boots over his swollen feet. Walking seemed out of the question, so Sprouse resigned himself to the fate of a straggler.

Cloud noted his friend's predicament and went to work. "Don't waste your time," Sprouse advised. "Just look up my wife and family when you get back, O.K.?"

Already Cloud was ripping Sprouse's boots from top to toe on a sharp edge in the shelter. Next he placed the split-open boots over Sprouse's feet and bound the tops with shoestrings. Only then did he speak.

"I'll say it again, Ted," Cloud said sternly. "We'll both make it out or we'll both stay! And I intend to make it out!"

He pulled Sprouse to his feet and hailed another prisoner

Satellite view of POW Camp #5, taken later after satellite pictures became available.

to help them outside. With arms draped over shoulders of comrades, Sprouse managed to shuffle his feet over the icy roadtop. Over the next four days, Ted concentrated on staying upright and advancing one step at a time. The second man periodically switched off, but Cloud never left Sprouse's side.

For supper, Cloud would bring Sprouse's handful of corn, usually seasoning it with a quip, such as, "You got it pretty good, Ted. Not only do I pull you along all day, but I feed you, too."

Sprouse admitted he had it "pretty good," but he wished he was less a burden. Not only did his legs and feet hurt constantly, but walking with upraised arms all day long aggravated his back no end. But looking around, he saw others slogging along in pain and misery as well. And there was the remarkable Corporal Roe. This plucky nineteen-year-old was now hiking along unassisted, a miraculous recovery, indeed.

On January 25th, 1951, some 3400 American and Allied prisoners reached Chinese Prison Camp Number 5 near Pyoktong, North Korea. They had endured unspeakable treatment and privation on the six-week twisting march. Perhaps now they would receive Red Cross parcels, mail, food, medicine and protection under provisions of the Geneva Conventions. Chances of survival were much better now, surely. As a matter of historical record, however, most would not survive another month—let alone the war's duration.

VI
PRISON WITHOUT WALLS

The Yalu River flowed around Camp 5 on three sides. Since Chinese guards shut off the only land exit, enclosing walls were not necessary. This arrangement was intentional, of course, for UN spotter planes would have picked up telltale prison outlines.

"Getting out should be easy," Sprouse confided to Don Cloud shortly after arrival.

"But what would we do then?" Cloud mused.

"We'll have to think about that, Don."

Such optimism was premature; Cloud and Sprouse would need all their cunning and resourcefulness just to stay alive in weeks ahead. Because they were able to walk, they found themselves among those dragging rice mats laden with deceased Americans across the frozen Yalu to a flood plain in Manchuria. There, in frozen soil, they scratched out shallow common graves to accommodate a daily toll of some forty expired prisoners. This grim task constantly reminded Sprouse that the margin between living and dying was narrowing by the day.

Sprouse could accept the passing of those he didn't know, but burying one of "his" men—twelve of the nineteen captured together would succumb—was another matter. And the interment of Corporal Don Roe was absolutely devastating. It seemed terribly ironic that the plucky Roe should die from dysentery after his heroic struggle to make it to Camp 5. And it was maddening that Roe succumbed for want of a little food, medicine, and rest that should have been provided by captors.

Although Chinese guards seemed callous and brutal, Sprouse learned there were exceptions. For instance, when they buried Corporal Roe the guard turned away while Sprouse, Cloud and a couple others paused to pray. Perhaps this guard concluded Christian ritual would not be interfered with in this particular case—whatever the penalty!

Another perplexing experience was more to the point. Sprouse and Cloud were boiling filched potatoes one day when a guard nicknamed "Scarface" came to investigate the smoke. He took in the scene immediately, wagged his finger and said "No good!" Instead of halting the illegal act, however, Scarface walked away.

Sprouse and Cloud concluded he was off to report the infraction so they gulped down half-cooked potatoes. As long as they were to be punished, why not consume the loot! When nothing happened, Sprouse and Cloud went to investigate. Lo and behold! Scarface was acting as lookout, making sure other guards did not interfere.

Over ensuing months, Sprouse learned more of Scarface's background. He had been interned during Japan's occupation of China in World War II. When he wouldn't co-operate, Japanese soldiers slit his throat from ear to ear. An American doctor, probably a missionary, found the mutilated Chinaman and sewed him back together as best he could. Out of spite, Scarface joined communist opposition but even-tually found himself in Korea guarding Americans to whom he felt indebted.

Sprouse concluded Scarface was a decent human being doing the best he could to solve his dilemma. "He was the best of all the guards we had in captivity," said Sprouse. "By far!"

The haphazard burials reminded Sprouse of his brother Rex. Without a doubt, obstacles to identifying remains in postwar Korea would be insurmountable. Common graves, no dog tags, no markings of any kind. And that was assuming graves would be undisturbed! How could exhumed wartime dead ever be repatriated with assurance they had been reliably identified? Granted, World War II records undoubtedly had been better kept, but Sprouse was content with his family's decision to leave Rex buried among fallen comrades at St. Avold.

Given the paltry diet and continued exposure to harsh elements, dysentery raged uncontrollably among prisoners all that winter. Some didn't bother to wear trousers because trips to the latrine were so frequent and bowel movements so spontaneous. Better sanitation would have helped control the epidemic, but a decent diet would have been the best remedy. The daily handful of corn, soybeans or rice contributed the bare minimum for survival, an intentional strategy no doubt. Healthy prisoners would be more likely to resist captors and to attempt escape, wouldn't they?

Nonetheless, resolute prisoners did not give in. When someone suggested charcoal would alleviate dysentery symptoms, Sprouse and Cloud began chewing charred wood pulled from cooking fires. "Medicine" or placebo, the raw dose of carbon seemed effective.

Not surprising, prisoner morale deteriorated into a dog-eat-dog culture in Camp 5 where all ranks intermingled. Captors had encouraged a breakdown in cohesion by stripping all dignity and semblance of rank from officers and NCOs who were still legally obligated to lead. Everyone was now equal. Without discipline, stronger prisoners began taking advantage of weaker ones in a frantic contest to survive. "Rats" and "progressives" soon were betraying fellow prisoners in order to curry favor with communists, who would reward them with food and cigarettes.

"Loners" who had no one to turn to in a crisis were the most vulnerable; consequently, a prisoner would team up with someone he could trust. Sprouse and Cloud were typical in this respect. When Sprouse had been ready to give up, Cloud literally had hauled him into Camp 5 and nursed him back to his feet. Then it was Sprouse's turn.

When Don Cloud came down with pneumonia a few weeks later, his chances of surviving without nourishment, medicine, rest and comfort seemed hopeless. In desperation, Sprouse boiled pine needles and forced Cloud to drink the acrid brew. Next, Sprouse contributed his own daily ration and forced Cloud to eat the tasteless gruel. As for himself, Sprouse stayed alive by retrieving soybeans spilled from carts along a trail near the river. Not a morsel escaped his sharp eyes.

"I could spot a little tan bean on stony soil twenty yards away," he recalled later.

Sprouse knew from boyhood days that soybeans were rich in protein, but he now learned they were tasty if parched. When Cloud was able to walk again, both would go to the cart trail and gather soybeans or other discarded foodstuffs to supplement their daily handout of grain. Whether items were spoiled made little difference, for as Sprouse surmised, "We're more apt to die from starvation than rotten food." In such fashion they were able to maintain a semblance of health, even improve slightly.

Another affliction proved more stubborn, however. Sprouse, suffering from the aftereffects of frozen feet, forced himself to walk in order to stimulate circulation. By so doing, he hoped his lower extremities would heal themselves. His resolve had intensified as he observed GI medics treat others with similar conditions.

When pain became unbearable, a medic would scrape away decayed flesh with a piece of broken glass—or he would amputate the member altogether. No painkillers, no antiseptics. Yet the primitive surgery often worked, for once a toe had been scraped or removed the patient usually improved. But not always, of course, and the patient would now be minus part of his foot.

Not to denigrate the aidmen's efforts; they were doing the best they could under the circumstances and with the training they had received. At that stage, the reds wouldn't allow captured doctors to ply their skill, because they couldn't be trusted to treat the "right" captives. Like everything else, medical care was reserved for those who would cooperate with Marxists.

So Sprouse avoided treatment, even though his feet and legs hurt constantly. At times—usually at night—his shin bones felt like they were being scraped by a sharp knife. Tears would fill his eyes as he fought to retain composure. An empathic Don Cloud would massage Sprouse's lower limbs in an attempt to bring relief.

"We're going to make it, Ted" he would insist at such times.

A Darwinian twist also brought reassurance. Prisoners who survived the first dreadful month began to adapt to their harsh environment. Then, too, a modicum of stability crept into camp life as guards settled into a rigid, predictable routine. At times Sprouse waxed hopeful about the future. That's when his thoughts turned to his wife, his little son, and his family.

He would wonder what they had been told. Probably that Ted Sprouse was "missing in action." His brother Don would explain the term to them. What would they make of it? Ted doubted communists had notified anyone of his capture.

Indeed, these "animals" would do nothing to alleviate concerns—even of loved ones back home!

Sprouse had sent no letters in months. How could he? Neither had he received any mail—any word at all! Why, some tragedy could have befallen his wife, son, or family.

Of course, he had no idea how the war was going: who was winning, who was losing. But he knew that his fate surely hung on the outcome of battles. Living in this limbo of uncertainty tempted Sprouse to believe no one cared, no one was working in behalf of these miserable wretches in Camp 5 near Pyoktong, North Korea. Such was the impact of not knowing anything.

Actually, attempts were being made to reach American prisoners in North Korea. But progress depended on cooperation between belligerents, a capricious variable when dealing with wily communists.

When war broke out in June 1950, the International Committee of the Red Cross had appealed for both sides to abide by the Geneva Conventions. United Nations powers readily agreed, and so did North Korea—but through the United Nations in New York. The nuance was significant inasmuch as it indicated the communists were keeping Red Cross at arm's length. Still, North Korea did release two lists of the first Americans captured that summer, when the war was going in its favor.

After the Inchon landing, however, the enemy's mood changed. When the American Red Cross tried to distribute food parcels to prisoners of war in North Korea, it was stymied completely. The International Red Cross approached China's Red Cross Society as intermediary, but the Chinese said they could not interfere with North Korea's sovereignty. This was a ploy, of course, for even after China entered the war that fall its Red Cross Society would not cooperate. Thus, nothing could be done for captured Americans—until the communists found it advantageous to cooperate.

In July 1951, a year after the war's beginning, the door opened a crack. General MacArthur had been replaced as commander-in-chief in the Far East by General Matthew B. Ridgway. MacArthur had been insubordinate to President Truman and the Joint Chiefs of Staff in wanting to go all out to win the war. With his removal, a more moderate approach could be taken.

Although armistice negotiations soon began at Kaesong and raised hopes, there would be no breakthrough. Rather, Communists needed time to wrench every possible concession from UN negotiators—and to "prepare" captives they held in North Korea. In the meantime, Ted Sprouse, Don Cloud and others struggled along emotionally isolated—as did their loved ones at home.

Four months after capture, Ted Sprouse discovered "luxury" is relative. By April 5th the weather was warm enough for prisoners to bathe in the Yalu River. The water was still icy cold and they had no soap, but prisoners used sand to scour away months of filth and rid skinny bodies of vermin.

To complete the task, prisoners boiled water in makeshift containers and tossed lice-infested garments into the cauldron. They cheered as dead insects bubbled to the surface. While clothing dried in the sun, prisoners roamed naked on the river bank. At sundown they pulled on still-damp garments—but they were clean and lice free. Luxury indeed!

A downside was the shock prisoners experienced upon beholding their emaciated bodies. Those with beriberi could hardly walk from grotesquely swollen testicles; others had ankles larger than thighs. "Skin stretched over bones," Sprouse thought aloud. Cloud added a solemn note: "Reminds me of

Holocaust survivors at the end of World War II." Then conversation lightened a bit.

"Ted, you don't look like a big league prospect to me."

"Maybe I'm faster now," Sprouse retorted.

"Not on those 'wheels' you ain't, ol' buddy!"

Cloud's voice trailed off. Mirth under the circumstances was a fleeting mood. A prisoner need only glance northward toward the graveyard across the river to be reminded of his vulnerability. Any day he, too, might join the multitude gathering there. Small wonder the death rate spiked upward in days following the "bath."

"Some just lay down and died to get it over with," Sprouse—who guessed he weighed about 100 pounds, down from 180—recalled.

But the hardy still carried on, even helping those suffering from "give-up-itis." Besides joking to lighten somberness, remedies extended to force-feeding comrades, even if it meant prying their mouths open or scooping up spit-out food and shoving it down resisting throats. Another trick was to goad a lethargic prisoner into fighting back. Once on his feet, he oftentimes came around and started functioning again.

Others seized upon any opportunity for diversion. Someone copped a pair of scissors and started "haircut day." Prisoners hacked away at each other's beards and shoulder-length locks with creative enthusiasm. Appearances changed, of course, and sometimes names as well.

Thereafter, Sprouse was nicknamed "Pop." Serious mannerisms lent a mature impression to everything about Ted. With a full beard, he looked much older than his early twenties. Add a somewhat crippled gait due to pain of frost-bitten feet and Pop seemed a fitting nickname.

Although prisoners had no way of knowing, the worst of the physical ordeal was over. Of 2730 American deaths in

Korean prison camps, only nineteen would occur after the first winter. Of course, by the spring of 1951 the most seriously wounded and weakened had expired. Then, too, survivors had become more savvy. Finally, captors began treating them somewhat better, allowing American doctors to treat fellow prisoners, for example. Surprisingly, tobacco was handed out to smokers now and then, as well.

Rations added up to about 1200 calories a day, the minimum for survival. Corn, maize, or millet seeds were the staples through the week. On Sundays, prisoners usually received rice, more nutritious and digestible than other grains. Infrequently, they were given a bit of pork for added protein. More importantly, prisoners now knew how to bend camp rules when an opportunity presented itself.

Korean civilians often passed through Camp 5. When Sprouse and Cloud met one carrying eggs in elongated woven containers one evening, they bought five eggs and a box of matches with the $90 they had concealed from captors. They smuggled the eggs back to their hooch where they boiled them over a forbidden fire. The fresh eggs were savored that night and over the next couple days.

Other procurements were less delightful, however. Once they coaxed a cat into their hut, then slaughtered and dressed out the carcass. Cloud conjectured that cat would taste something like squirrel or rabbit, both of which they remembered from boyhood hunting days. Although they cooked and downed the meal, both ate squeamishly.

"Not as good as squirrel by a long shot," was Cloud's summation.

Actually, cat was better than scrawny sparrows they later trapped and cooked out of desperation—even though tiny birds were a Korean delicacy. Through such creativity in procuring food, Sprouse and Cloud managed to grow stronger and to build up a small reserve of foodstuffs.

When a barge loaded with potatoes tied up along the riverbank, prisoners were elated at the prospect. Knowing they would be sent to unload the cargo, they began plotting to garner a share. Led by Sprouse and Cloud, prisoners moved a large rock aside behind their hut. Then they scooped out the depression by carrying handfuls of dirt away in coat pockets. When the excavation was completed, the rock was rolled back into place.

Prisoners managed to carry off the ruse that night. They smuggled potatoes inside clothing and stowed them under the rock, aided by a planned commotion to distract guards. All had gone smoothly—or so it seemed.

At roll call, an interpreter appeared alongside the guard. Sprouse was accused of stealing potatoes from the Korean people. He denied knowing anything about such a crime. Coyly, the interpreter led him to the rock. Guards rolled it away, exposing the cache of potatoes. Without a doubt, captured GIs had been betrayed by a fellow prisoner.

Cloud, believing things would be easier for Sprouse if the guilt were spread around, volunteered that he had been in on the enterprise. His confession was readily accepted and the twosome were ushered to headquarters. There they were made to stand, contemplating their pending fate, throughout an extremely hot day. Then they were punished!

In a somewhat formal proceeding, both were accused of not only stealing potatoes but of planning an escape. Both denied the latter charge and eventually convinced the senior communist they just wanted more food. They were sentenced to carrying "honeybuckets" (latrine-slop containers) out into the fields for thirty days. Actually, the Reds were not far off the mark. Sprouse and Cloud were stashing food for an eventual break out; however, potatoes were too bulky and perishable to be included.

Changes within camp 5 usually reflected developments elsewhere. By June 1951, a stalemate had settled along the approximate pre-war boundary. Communist strategy now shifted to diplomacy and a rancorous battle for world opinion. Americans prisoners of war soon would be blue chips in this evolving poker game; however, prisoners didn't have a clue as to what was happening.

Out of the blue one day, Ted Sprouse was summoned to headquarters for interrogation. Any tactical information he may have had when captured was out of date, so Ted was confident he could no longer aid and abet the enemy's cause. He was startled to learn that he was now accused of "war crimes" against the peace-loving Korean people. In such fashion, Sprouse was introduced to "brainwashing."

This first session went on for thirty-six hours. Sprouse was made to stand at attention throughout. He was given no food or water, although his inquisitors ate, drank and smoked freely in front of him. Every four hours a fresh inquisitor took over and hammered away. When Sprouse asked to go to the latrine, he was allowed to go eventually—even nature's call was used to apply pressure.

Sprouse stuck to his basic training guidance throughout the ordeal: If you become a prisoner of war, give only your name, rank, serial number, and date of birth. Doggedly he clung to this mandate. When he was called a "running dog of capitalism," Sprouse shook his head in disbelief. When asked if he committed atrocities against "peace-loving" Koreans, he shook his ahead again. When asked why he had fired "germ-laden shells" into Korean villages, he merely shrugged. How ridiculous could they be?

Although one frustrated inquisitor threatened to hit him, Sprouse was not physically abused during brainwashing. So, he rightly concluded he was being measured for susceptibil-

70

ity to new ideas. When the session ended, communists told Sprouse he had been treated "leniently." As parting gifts, they gave him a Marxist pamphlet and John Steinbeck's *Grapes of Wrath* to read—and contemplate.

Don Cloud's experience was similar, as were his conclusions. "Once you say something, they'll never leave you alone," he whispered to Sprouse confidentially. "And if you ever wrote anything out, they'd never let up on you afterwards."

Sprouse agreed as he contemplated the reading materials given him. "Funny they can get anti-American books and the *Daily Worker* for us to read but nothing else," he mused.

"They could if they wanted to, Ted."

Cloud and Sprouse had stuck to the rules, but they were atypical. Word soon circulated that prisoners were giving in, writing confessions and signing peace petitions. Sprouse concluded there were three groups: Some went all out to cooperate, even denouncing their country and were called "progressives." Some just went along to get by. And some fought back, arguing with the Reds and were called "reactionaries." The upshot of this fragmenting was that a prisoner didn't know whom to trust—for a while at least.

Of course, there was a lot of confusion. Brainwashing was a new technique developed by the communists during Chairman Mao's revolution. At the time, interrogators ruthlessly attempted to disintegrate the minds of Chiang Kai-shek's Kuomintang soldiers so they could be recruited into the Red Army. It was part of the overall plan to redistribute land and resources throughout China.

In Korea, the goal was a bit different. By isolating UN prisoners, they could be more easily controlled. Next, prisoners would be recruited to distribute communist propaganda when they eventually returned home. Finally, communists sought to actively convert a few to their cause, the purpose of whom would soon become apparent.

Even though most prisoners came from modest backgrounds, they tended to consider brainwashing a "bunch of malarkey." How could anyone be taken in by such nonsense? And it was true that communists soon gave up on Sprouse and his ilk, so slight were prospects of their serving a useful role. But brainwashing still had an impact on even the stalwart.

The sowing of distrust has already been mentioned. Then there was the fallout from mental stress. After a particular grueling session, Sprouse found himself "blind as a bat" when darkness fell. This was shocking because Sprouse had always had good night vision before. Now Cloud had to lead him around at night, even on trips to the latrine. Strangely, his vision in daylight was not affected. The impairment was to continue throughout the remainder of his time as a prisoner.

Once the reds gave up on Sprouse, Cloud and other reactionaries, they were sent into the woods on logging details. "Your airplanes destroyed homes and bridges so you must now make repairs," was the rationale served up. Truth to tell, Sprouse preferred laboring to the interrogations and educational sessions on Marxism. Not that the work wasn't arduous, of course.

The first week they dropped trees, trimmed branches and cut logs of specified lengths. The following week, they carried logs six miles back to camp. Since Sprouse's back was still pained, Cloud shouldered most of the two-man loads. At day's end, they would be totally exhausted, but their minds were clear and their consciences at peace.

Late summer in 1951 brought a new pestilence. Prisoners at first attributed stomach pains to faulty diet, but when someone expelled a foot-long worm in his stools the culprit had been identified. Shortly, everyone found traces of worms in his latrine visits. Drinking hot water brought some relief by flushing out the pencil-like parasites. Of course, such treatment did nothing to purge intestines completely.

For a permanent cure, Ted Sprouse turned to a remedy once suggested by Grandpa Jim Sprouse. When asked why he chewed tobacco, Grandpa Sprouse had replied that doing so prevented worms. Now Ted took a generous chew, masticated it thoroughly, and swallowed the glob. He vomited afterwards, but no worms came up. The attempted cure proved worse than the condition, however.

Sprouse became so ill that he went into delirium. During one hallucination, Cloud dangled a piece of cabbage before Sprouse's opened mouth and enticed worms to emerge one at a time. Sprouse counted twenty-eight exiting before a particularly large one gagged and choked him. He awoke in a frenzy and with a paralysis so pervasive he could barely move.

Cloud persuaded the guard that Sprouse was unable to work that day. After a cursory check the guard grunted approval, so Sprouse stayed on the floor of the hooch wrapped up in his overcoat. Cloud slipped Sprouse the small bag of foodstuffs they had managed to hoard in case he felt like eating later.

A progressive had observed the transaction, however. After Sprouse dozed off, the progressive crept near with a knife in hand. When he grabbed for the food, Sprouse snapped out of his lethargy and kicked out in self-defense. Then all hell broke loose.

Cloud had suspected treachery was afoot and returned. He struck the progressive with a brick, knocking him senseless. Sprouse believed Cloud would have killed the predator had he not been stopped. As it was, Cloud made his point and the progressive slinked away and never reported the altercation.

That prisoners would kill for food was an indication of their obsession with things to eat. Not surprisingly, bull sessions often centered on food fantasies. Sprouse fancied pancakes splashed with butter and syrup. Others yearned for ice cream in a variety of flavors and with exquisite sauces; one relished vanilla topped with mustard! Cloud and "Jack" Jackson thought sardines covered with chocolate might be a fitting dessert.

Infrequently, prisoners had something different for their meals in Camp 5. While unloading fish one night, Sprouse and Cloud feasted on the move. When it grew light, they were taken aback by the sight of maggots swarming over the fish. Other than gagging at the thought, neither Cloud nor Sprouse suffered any adverse consequences, however.

As death rates dropped, a man's passing became more significant. And if he were unusual, more so. Such was the case when the "newsman" died that summer. Ted had never learned his real name, but then "newsman" was not forthcoming about anything.

It seems he had been a news reporter before joining the United States Army, a background that gave him a unique slant on being a prisoner of war. Both analytical and adept at recording details, he somehow managed to preserve his notes throughout the twisting march and first few months in Camp 5. A "rat" once turned him in for subversive activities, but "newsman" never revealed his secrets to interrogators. Consequently, he died with his story still unwritten.

Sprouse found little consolation in "newsman's" passing with secrecy intact, however. Better that he had lived to detail for Americans the fraud China's lenient policy truly was. A dramatic first-person account would deflate blatant propaganda now being spewed out by communist negotiators. Ted Sprouse was quite sensitive at the time, for he had been recently victimized by Chinese propagandists.

Curiosity had piqued when several wounded prisoners were summoned to headquarters. Sprouse, who was one of them, was astounded when Chinese medics dressed his open-sored feet in gleaming white bandages. They even affixed a sling around his neck to relieve his injured back. All the while, Chinese medics were most solicitous of his comfort and wellbeing.

Other prisoners were being similarly treated. What did this abrupt change mean? What did it portend? As always, no explanation was given.

Then the group was marched out of camp 5 a couple miles, turned around and headed back. Ahead Ted saw movie cameras being put in place along the road. Then he saw other prisoners being arranged along the way as a welcoming committee. Close up he recognized known "rats" and "progressives" among the group, which now broke out in cheers and applause. Ted's contingent had been "welcomed" into prisoner-of-war camp by fellow Americans, and the scene was now on film!

When it dawned on prisoners they had been used for a propaganda movie, they broke away. Some shouted and used gestures the communists could not mistake. Surprisingly, the communists reacted slowly and tentatively; they were thrown on the defensive for the moment.

Perhaps this novel exposure to critical scrutiny not only gave the Chinese pause, but it may have sown the first seeds of doubt in minds of die-hard communists. Certainly, outside influences were just beginning to penetrate communist culture ever so slightly. The thought must have occurred to at least some propagandists that they, too, lived within a "prison without walls."

VII
ESCAPING

In summer's warmth, prisoners grew more hopeful—
and restless! All were tempted in one way or another to break
out of this odious culture that turned men into animals. They
yearned desperately for a normal life—whatever the cost! But
by then, of course, captors had rendered most prisoners physically incapable of escaping and many emotionally so as well.

Although Sprouse initially thought they would have little
trouble in breaking away, plans had to be shelved because of
debilitation and extremely cold weather. He and Cloud had
been forced to concentrate on just lasting out the winter. Still,
Sprouse and Cloud never abandoned the idea of escaping, so
they planned and schemed patiently. Of course, they were
not alone in this respect.

Throughout long months, prisoners sought to escape in
a variety of ways. As mentioned, the easiest way out that first
winter had been simply to lie down and freeze to death—and
many did just that. Some took an opposite approach, drawing
on hatred and bitterness for energy in fighting back at tormentors.

The soldier who lost a finger because he was slow in
removing his wedding band shortly after capture never for-
gave the "gooks." Seething rage kept him going, invigorated
him. One spring day a guard dared to prod him—and got the
surprise of his life! The prisoner punched the guard squarely
in the face. As expected, retribution was swift and brutal.

Guards tied the prisoner's hands behind his back, hoisted
him to a rafter until his toes barely touched the ground, and
then left him suspended. Once a day the culprit was lowered
to eat and relieve himself, then back to his toes he went. Pre-

sumably after seven days he had learned a lesson, so he was let down. Surprise again! He punched the first guard within striking distance. This time he was tossed into a hole in the ground and covered over. When let out several days later, the incorrigible prisoner punched the first guard he encountered.

"The poor guy spent a lot of time in solitary," Sprouse recalled ruefully. "I believe he really wanted them to shoot him—sort of like suicide."

A prisoner named Presley was more ingenious—and certainly more fortunate! A trusted friend of Sprouse, Presley cooked up a concoction of greens gathered in Korean fields during work details and ate them along with his handful of corn. "Balancing my diet," he explained. That night he became violently ill and apparently died from food poisoning. When Sprouse listened for a heartbeat the next morning, he could hear nothing. A GI Medic confirmed the finding and covered Presley's body as was customary when a prisoner expired.

When they returned from roll call, however, Presley was walking about in confused state. The spell lasted several days, with Presley mechanically following camp routine without speaking. Eventually he came around to more normal behavior, whereupon he claimed he had seen "another world."

He described heaven in awe-inspiring terms. He told of enchantingly beautiful music played by angels during his out-of-body experience. More convincing, however, was the man's changed attitude. Now he blissfully accepted a prisoner's lot, as if he could tolerate "a few inconveniences" knowing the glory that awaited him eventually.

Sprouse was skeptical, even teased his friend about hallucinating because of "bad weeds," but Presley never wavered in his account nor his positivity. Perhaps God had touched this wretched soul with a glimpse of Paradise. Who was to deny the possibility? Ultimately, Sprouse concluded Presley had indeed managed to escape worldly misery in phenomenal fashion.

Others sought "salvation" through another medium. Knowledgeable prisoners spotted hemp plants while on work detail and pocketed the leaves. Later they rolled the "pot" in newspaper and puffed away. Some found this outlet highly satisfactory and walked around in constant euphoria while the marijuana lasted. Apparently they had found an ideal escape under the circumstances—but maybe not! Sprouse wondered if they had begun a habit that carried over upon return to the States.

Demons of many stripes thrived within the oppressive camp culture. One was guilt, guilt over having been captured or for not having tried another path of avoidance. At one time or another, every prisoner in Camp 5 pondered what might have been. They second-guessed options they had chosen in the midst of battlefield panic. Most kept such thoughts to themselves, but some spoke out to reveal haunting concerns.

One night several prisoners from the 38th Field Artillery discussed the fateful ambush south of Kunuri. Typically, Sprouse and Cloud listened as others unburdened themselves. One voice sounded familiar, but the speaker's face was obscured by darkness. He said that everyone had taken off and he was left alone to do what had to be done. He described in detail how he went from howitzer to howitzer, destroying each in turn by dropping a thermite grenade down the tube. Of course, by doing so he sacrificed his own chance of escape and the enemy ultimately subdued him.

"But my conscience is clear," he concluded philosophically. "The Chinks never had those guns to use against other Americans."

When the group broke up, Sprouse caught a glimpse of

the speaker—a C Battery officer! Ted confronted him on the spot, reminded him that he was nowhere in sight during the losing battle. Furthermore, C Battery NCOs had not only destroyed the howitzers but had led remnants of artillerymen in the attempt to escape.

The officer said nothing in return and shuffled off into the night. Later, upon reflection, Sprouse felt less harshly; the forlorn guy had indulged such fantasy to escape a personal demon—if only for a few minutes in supposed anonymity.

When peace talks got underway in early June 1951, the Chinese brought new prisoners into Camp 5. Actually, the arrivals were "old" prisoners who had undergone torture and brainwashing across the river. Reportedly, some had made radio broadcasts, diatribes against the United States government. Now they were being returned so they could be released when a peace agreement was reached. Not knowing facts, prisoners in Camp 5 gave arrivals benefit of the doubt.

When peace talks faltered, however, the Chinese decided to take these same prisoners back north, perhaps to use them again as propaganda spokesmen. But other prisoners in Camp 5 objected, even went on strike. They refused to fall out for roll call, an act surely to bring retribution. For three days the standoff continued, whereupon the Chinese called off their plan. They did not want to risk unfavorable attention at that particular time, but there was another reason prisoners had won out.

When it appeared peace might be achieved, the Chinese had "fattened up" prisoners for obvious reasons. They were given rice twice a day three times a week. Occasionally, they were given a small piece of pork as well. Although captors were just being pragmatic, prisoners benefited nonetheless. They not only grew stronger but they became more defiant, dared to take a stand, and had gotten away with it.

When peace talks stalled, however, rations were cut back and psychological pressure increased once more. The communist explanation of the failed negotiations revealed what this mind game was all about.

"They don't want you back!" the interpreter proclaimed. "United Nations forces torture thousands of Chinese and Korean prisoners on Koje-do, but they won't exchange them for you—not even one! Your government has again forsaken you! But you should have expected as much, for capitalist governments are corrupt and must be removed. Only then will you be truly free! So join peace-loving peoples of the world and work unceasingly for peace."

The blurb was repeated over and over, of course, and bitterness grew among UN prisoners. More Americans turned progressive and wrote articles condemning leaders who had sent them to fight this "criminal" war. Some accused the United States government of exploiting the poor and disadvantaged back home. Peace petitions circulated freely and many signed, if only to vent frustration. Newspapers written and edited by UN prisoners began to circulate regularly with peace messages. The communists were making headway.

Distressing, too, was the abrupt departure of seventeen prisoners who were removed in the dead of night and were observed being taken into Manchuria. Sprouse assumed they had been recruited as propagandists, but another fate may have befallen them. Soviet dissidents in the post-Cold War era disclosed American prisoners had been sent to the Soviet Union for "experimentation." Whatever the case, the seventeen never returned to Camp 5.

Along with the others, Sprouse and Cloud found themselves deeply discouraged. They had gone through the most wrenching emotional ordeal possible, only to have their hopes cruelly shattered. They were back at square one with no relief in sight.

Even nature seemed to conspire against them. While they bathed in the Yalu River one afternoon, a sudden storm forced Sprouse and Cloud to leave the water. As they dressed hurriedly, a lightning bolt knocked both to the ground. Otherwise they were uninjured, but a nearby Korean boy was killed outright. Sprouse came away with increased gratitude to Almighty God—and renewed respect for the awesomeness of lightning!

With prospects for release so dimmed at mid-summer, Sprouse decided it was time to escape. Both he and Cloud were feeling healthy again and their plans were completed. Warm weather would enable them to survive in light prison garb. They had a supply of corn and soybeans to sustain them for a couple weeks, after which they would forage food en route. They would drink from streams without concern, for they had long ago become immune to Korean pestilences. It was now or never!

They were somewhat encouraged by the attempt of an American lieutenant, Tommy Trexler, who had earlier gotten away for a month. Eventually, sickness had forced him to seek help from a Korean family who turned him in. But Sprouse and Cloud would avoid that pitfall by supporting each other, and by crossing into Manchuria where people might be less hostile—maybe even sympathetic.

Once across the river, they would follow the Yalu westward to open sea. Perhaps along the way they could attract attention of UN planes that might assist in rescuing the escapees. Failing that, they would continue to the Yellow Sea, steal a boat and push off towards UN vessels operating along the Korean coast. A long shot without a doubt, but it might just work!

Sprouse and Cloud picked a night of torrential rain to slip down to the river's edge. They shed clothing and wrapped everything in a GI poncho before pushing out into the current. Cloud, the stronger swimmer, helped Sprouse along and they reached the far side—Manchuria! They dressed quickly and started westward, already exhilarated by a taste of freedom.

Suddenly forms loomed ahead in the rain and darkness. The escapees were ordered to halt or be shot. They had been betrayed by a "rat" who had seen Sprouse and Cloud depart. Of course, captors were already vigilant on this stormy night, and they moved quickly to head off the escapees.

Sprouse and Cloud were hauled back across the river and paraded through camp—an example for others with foolish ideas. The trial lasted an entire day, as they were accused and harangued endlessly. Then they were sentenced to three months in isolation. Isolation it was, for they never left the cave—even to relieve themselves. So ingloriously ended their dream of breaking away.

Paradoxically, others gained release in that very same storm. Heavy rains caused the Yalu River to flood the Manchurian plain where Americans lay buried. Roily waters caught up shallow coverings and swept remains down river and out into the Yellow Sea. Thus, in poetic fashion the deceased "escaped"; however, the irony was of little consolation to those still in captivity.

When released from isolation, Sprouse and Cloud settled back into prison routine. They would be closely watched from then on, so another escape attempt was out of the question. They had no choice but to resign themselves to making the best of the situation until released—whenever.

In the meantime, more prisoners continued to arrive, either having just been captured or shifted from another camp.

"Pluto," so-called because he wore his pile-lined cap with one flap up and one down reminiscent of the Disney canine's ears, was one of these. He was carried into Sprouse's hut with an open bullet hole clean through his chest. He was able to breath only if both openings of the sucking wound were sealed. Of lesser importance, he had been shot through the knee as well. His chances of survival were slim, indeed.

But other prisoners rallied around Pluto. If his breathing stopped, they would give mouth-to-mouth resuscitation and revive him. They also fed and bathed him. Surprisingly, Pluto had a cheery outlook. He was determined to recover and pushed himself to the limits. Soon he was on his feet and walking, progress that revealed a knee that "clacked like a typewriter." Bone fragments caused the sound, but the eerie condition did not deter Pluto.

"I'm happy to be alive," he quipped goodnaturedly. "Everything else I can handle."

"After that display, how could any of us feel sorry for ourselves?" Sprouse asked rhetorically.

The Turks offered another example of raw courage. Despite communist efforts to destroy all cohesion, Turk officers and NCOs maintained command of subordinates. As a result, the Turks could take a stand on occasion—and get away with it!

While Turks were bathing in the river one day, one started swimming away. Frenzied guards threatened to shoot him, so he nonchalantly returned to the group. Guards sought to pull him out for punishment, but first they had to catch him. All Turks swarmed around the culprit, leaving the guards a choice of punishing all or none. Expediently, frustrated guards chose the latter course.

At times the Turks could be brutal, however. The only Turk to die in Camp 5 was done in by his own countrymen.

The rogue had denounced his comrades and country during brainwashing, but he never benefited from his treachery. The traitor was found hanged with his throat cut in a warehouse where Turks worked. The Chinese let it go at that, perhaps appreciating the well-deserved outcome.

Concerns increased as winter approached. Would the second be a repeat of the first, when prisoners starved and froze to death by the hundreds? Collectively, they decided to cull their experience of intervening months and prepare. Of course, they were in better health going in, having recovered from ravages of the erstwhile death march. And they were encouraged by the fact that they had survived once before. Then, too, they had adjusted to camp culture, even enjoyed a bit of humor now and then to escape oppressive monotony.

A preposterous incident would buoy spirits, even though outcomes usually were at expense of the prisoners. For example, when a shipment of eggs arrived from China, prisoners looked forward to a dietary change. However, the eggs were rotten and GI cooks threw them out. Guards reacted furiously and reported the "waste" to headquarters. With straight face, an interpreter rebuked prisoners with a mind-boggling explanation:

"Your planes bombed the eggs while in transport, mixing yolks with whites. If you had waited, the yolks would have separated from the whites again. Now you have no eggs, stupid Americans!"

Although this particular rationale was ridiculous, communists were quite logical—once their sinister motives became clear. For instance, they unexpectedly turned over names of prisoners in Camp 5 to UN negotiators in mid-December 1951. Of course, they should have done so a year earlier, but the gesture would have served no purpose then. Now, through a seeming good-will act at Christmastime, communists appeared humane and reasonable before the world.

Regardless of such chicanery, prisoner news was deeply appreciated in American homes. Joanne Sprouse received a telegram on December 20th from the Secretary of the Army stating Ted's name was included in the list supplied by the enemy. Of course, she immediately informed the Sprouses in Drakesville.

CLASS OF SERVICE		1201	SYMBOLS
This is a full-rate Telegram or Cable-gram unless its de-ferred character is in-dicated by a suitable symbol above or pre-ceding the address.	**WESTERN UNION** W. P. MARSHALL, PRESIDENT		DL=Day Letter NL=Night Letter ◆ .T=Int'l Letter Telegram VLT=Int'l Victory Ltr.

The filing time shown in the date line on telegrams and day letters is STANDARD TIME at point of origin. Time of receipt is STANDARD TIME at point of destination

MB004 SPG549 KA566

K.LLA927 XV GOVT PD DUPE OF TGM SENT TO CBQ RR OFFICE CFM)=
WUX WASHINGTON DC 19 427P=
MRS JOANNE D SPROUSE,

1951 DEC 20 AM 8 21

    DLR IMMY=RTE TWO CENTERVILLE IOWA=

THE SECRETARY OF THE ARMY HAS ASKED ME TO INFORM YOU THAT
THE NAME SPROUSE TEDDY R. BELIEVED TO BE THAT OF YOUR
HUSBAND IS INCLUDED IN A LIST OF PRISONERS SUPPLIED BY
ENEMY FORCES. IT IS NOT YET VERIFIED AND NO ASSURANCE AS
TO ITS ACCURACY CAN BE GIVEN AT THIS TIME. WHEN IT IS
CERTAIN THAT THIS IS A TRUE LIST YOU WILL BE NOTIFIED AS
SOON AS POSSIBLE AND WITHOUT REQUEST ON YOUR PART=

WM E BERGIN MAJOR GENERAL USA THE ADJUTANT GENERAL=

Official notification of Sprouse's change to POW status, December, 1951, a year after his capture.

"It was the best possible Christmas gift," Shirley recalled. "Where there's life, there's hope."

But it would be another seven months before they actually heard from Ted. In late July three letters, dated January 13, February 11, and March 15, arrived in Centerville for Joanne. The letters had been postmarked in Canton, China.

Ted told the family not to worry because he was being

well treated by the Chinese. Further, he would come home just as soon as the United States government "permitted." Although letters were in Ted's handwriting, they had been addressed by someone else. An address was included so the family could write to Ted.

"We were never certain the letters were from Ted," Betty Zaerr later recalled. "Some things just didn't ring true, but we eagerly wrote back to him with the hope he would get mail."

As for Ted himself, back in December he had been told he could write whenever he wanted—but letters would be reviewed by captors. So, warily, he penned letters to his wife, parents and siblings. Of course, writing and having letters delivered were two different things, for reliability of the delivery system depended on vagaries of ongoing peace talks.

With obvious leverage on both prisoners and families back home, communists used both incoming and outgoing mail to advance their agenda. "Improper" letters would be tossed away while those praising captors or criticizing the United States would ensure prompt dispatch. Moroseness and complaining were useful tones in getting a letter on its way as well.

Incoming mail would be dangled before a forlorn prisoner. If he seemed likely to cooperate, a letter would be handed over. If a prisoner complained about lack of mail, a "friendly" communist would promise to investigate. After letting suspense build, the benefactor would produce a couple letters. The grateful prisoner would then be receptive to suggestions on how to keep mail flowing. A line here, a term there, and what possible harm could come of that? Not surprising, prisoners frequently went along just to communicate with wives, parents and friends.

Ted's letter to his parents in December 1952 illustrates

the care needed in selection of verbiage to satisfy the communists and still not be disloyal to America:

Dear Folks:

Well here I am again and I hope this finds you all as well as I am. I'm getting treated fine and if everything turns out O.K. I will be home before long. I sure would like for this war to come to an end so people could live as they want to.

I wrote Jo a letter yesterday and then I didn't think I would be able to write anymore, but we can write two. I also got a letter from Jo's sister, Ethel, in Moline, Ill., and she said they got good news before Christmas. I hope you had a nice one. We did. I also hear you are having a bad winter back there.

Well folks, I can't think of anymore to say now so I will close and hope everything will turn out for the best and don't worry about me for I will be O.K. for the Chinese are treating us just fine.

Tell everyone hello and not to grow too fast for I won't know them when I get home. I won't even know my son. From what I hear he is getting pretty big and fat as a butter ball. God bless all of you and be with you forever.

Love,
Your son Ted

Some prisoners made propaganda broadcasts over Peking Radio's "POWs Calling" in order to be seen and heard by families. Others signed peace petitions as a way of getting through. Of course, there were progressives who openly cooperated with the Chinese in order to get along more comfortably. Tellingly, during thirty-three months in captivity, Ted Sprouse received only four letters from his wife and family, and only a fraction of the letters he wrote ever were delivered.

When the Chinese concluded in spring of 1952 that UN negotiators were not yet ready to work out a peace agreement on communist terms, they decided to use prisoners in more telling ways. There would be no letup for Ted Sprouse and Don Cloud in this switch. In fact, the only bright spot would be in their remaining together—as Cloud so frequently predicted. Upon reflection, remaining together under the circumstances was in itself an escape from a much more dire condition.

VIII
SUBTLE MOVES

In early 1952, the Korean Conflict was deadlocked—as were prisoners of war! Belligerents squared off in vicinity of the 38th Parallel with soldiers burrowed into the earth reminiscent of World War I trench warfare. Even so, men died at a steady pace in battles at the Punchbowl, Heartbreak Ridge and Bloody Ridge. All the while, mortars, artillery and planes shelled and bombed in steady rhythm.

"Rats as big as cats" pervaded battle zones, preying on garbage of war. Rats nibbled at carcasses strewn among mountains and throughout valleys. Rats snuggled behind walls of hooches and among accouterment stored in caves, dumps and bunkers. Soldiers, hastily inoculated against plague, shot the varmints as a diversion.

Negotiations continued, now at Panmunjom where UN, North Korean and Chinese representatives huddled. Both sides wanted an armistice—but on respective terms. Of all things, prisoners of war were the bone of contention. Communists wanted all prisoners returned—by force if necessary. UN forces insisted on voluntary repatriation—prisoners would not be returned against their will. The dichotomy left little room for prisoners' immediate welfare, however.

Some 160,000 North Koreans and Chinese were in UN camps, including civilian internees, ROKs impressed into the NKPA, and former Chinese Nationalists impressed into the CCF. Communists had reason to believe many would refuse repatriation, an embarrassment that would reflect unfavorably on their ideology. On the other hand, UN forces believed their men held prisoner would choose repatriation—and freedom.

89

To finesse their dilemma, communists swung to a propaganda offensive. They accused the UN of engaging in germ warfare and produced downed American pilots who "admitted" as much. Now brainwashing was coming into play.

Communists dropped an even more sensational card in this novel game that spring. With thousands of enemy prisoners in UN camps off the southeast coast of Korea at Koje-do, the UN was getting by with enclosures designed for a fraction of the total. Hopefully, an end to the war would take care of temporary crowding. But communists continued to stall—and mustered their forces behind barbed wire.

Pak Sang Hyong had made his way to Koje-do by intentionally getting captured back in 1951. He arrived in an enlisted man's uniform, but Pak was a high-ranking communist with a mission. He organized prisoners and set up a communications network. He eventually took over compounds from within and paraded units before startled guards, fashioned knives from mess-kit handles and spears from tent poles. Pak's preparations were military, but his objective was political.

In May 1952, Pak drew world attention by capturing the Koje-do prison commander through a ruse. Well timed broadcasts from Pyongyang and Peking denounced "barbarous massacres" and "atrocities" within UN compounds. International Red Cross inspected and found "inadequacies," as straight-faced prisoners complained of Geneva Conventions violations. Ironically, UN forces found themselves on the defensive—even though International Red Crossers were barred from communist prison camps in North Korea!

Eighth Army combat units soon cleaned up Koje-do in June, but communists had won a victory. Not only had they raised questions on voluntary repatriation, but they had humiliated UN forces before the world. The fallout had consequences for captured Americans as well.

Communists now turned to prisoners in North Korea with a clear goal in mind. Brainwashers would persuade some to refuse repatriation, thereby offsetting the impact of expected refusals at Koje-do. Such a development would be more significant than "proven" charges of germ warfare, surely.

As the first step, communists segregated captured officers and NCOs—who tended to be reactionary—from lower ranks. So when Ted Sprouse, Don Cloud and several hundred others were roused out at 2 a.m. one August morning and marched to barges on the Yalu River, they had no idea how they fit into the scheme of things. No warning, no explanation, no consideration. It was standing-room only, with prisoners making space for those who had to urinate or defecate over the side. Four days and nights the barges lumbered up the Yalu to Camp 4, much farther north than Pyoktong.

Upon arrival, Sprouse and Cloud were put in a dwelling with wooden floors, a novelty in North Korea. They were to live among eighty others—forty coloreds and forty whites. They had to believe this was intentional, that the mixing of races would somehow serve communist purposes. But shrewd as they were, the reds had overlooked something.

President Harry Truman had started desegregation of the armed forces by executive order back in 1948. Although residual bigotry remained, professional soldiers had begun to accept coloreds and would subordinate personal feelings to accomplish a mission. Tellingly, it was a colored sergeant named Black who cleared the air for everyone on the spot.

"They're trying to get us to fight among ourselves so's they can pick up the pieces," the veteran NCO warned after calling them together. "We must not fall into their trap, whatever it takes! If whites want to fight whites, go to it! But whites don't fight coloreds. Coloreds can fight among themselves, but not whites! You understand?"

91

But communists went a step further to fan animosities. The first week coloreds were made to do heavy work while whites took it easy. When this inequity didn't spark resentment, roles were switched. Still, the scheme didn't work. In fact, the transparent communist tactic actually drove coloreds and whites together, thanks to professionalism of American NCOs.

Sprouse was heartened when Chinese held a group session, citing historic examples of racial discrimination in the United States. Sergeant Black told the Chinese to mind their own damned business! "What we do in America is up to us, and you should correct your own inequalities before lecturing us." Sprouse was proud to be an NCO in the United States Army as he witnessed this gutsy response.

Of course, this was but a minor setback as the communists played their subtle game. They turned up pressure, appointing monitors from among prisoners who would conduct classes. Monitors were usually progressives who claimed America started the war, castigated government officials for sending soldiers as cannon fodder, and criticized Wall Streeters for growing rich while soldiers were dying. That fellow prisoners would say such things was a bitter pill for reactionaries.

Sprouse was surprised one day to be handed a copy of *Towards Truth and Peace*, the Camp 5 newspaper. He learned later this prisoner-produced paper, which now included sports columns, book reviews, short stories, a mailbag, bridge and chess problems and instructions on playing the guitar, and, of course, international news, was being circulated in all North Korean prison camps. That lot of progressives had come a long way!

As Chinese sorted out those with the most promise, they worked intensively with a select few. Not only were these recruits freed from work details, but they were praised, given medical supplies, regular mail, better food, more cigarettes, hard candy or an item of warm clothing. But resisters—the Sprouses and the Clouds—were dismissed out of hand and sent back to hard labor.

And hard labor it was! They now cut larger and heavier logs than before. A single log would require three men to carry it back to camp. Fortunately, Sprouse still worked with Cloud and "Jack" Jackson who were in comparatively good health, so he managed to last day in and day out.

The chill of fall came earlier at Camp 4, a definite minus to the move north from Pyoktong. Sprouse and Cloud had to break ice in the river after roll call each morning to wash up. "The colder it got, the shorter the bathing sessions," Sprouse recalled. When temperatures dipped into the teens, they stopped bathing altogether. Sanitation became a hit-or-miss thing the remainder of that winter.

Despite hardships and lack of mail, Sprouse continued to write whenever he had a chance. On October 24th he dispatched the following to his wife:

> My Darling Jo and Steve,
>
> Honey, we got another chance to write and I will drop you a few lines to let you know that I'm just fine. All the other guys are just fine also. We are waiting for the day when we get home.
>
> I got your letter and pictures of you and Steve and I sure was glad to get them along with the letter. You both look good and I'm sure glad of it.
>
> Darling, I don't think I have told you but Darwin Hill of Stratford is here with us and is O.K. I'm sure Don Felby of Albia is home. I hope you get to see him.
>
> Did Don Stuchel from Albia get home? I sure hope so. Well, Darling, I will close for now and hope you and Steve will take care of yourselves as I am doing.

Tell everyone I am just fine and hope and pray to
see you all very soon. I will always be thinking and
praying for the day to come when we are together.

Love, Ted

In late November 1952, Sprouse and Cloud returned to Pyoktong—temporarily. The idea for a first Inter-Camp Olympics surely came from the International Olympic games held earlier that summer. Since communists weren't likely to entertain UN prisoners without a purpose, Sprouse was skeptical when he and Cloud were ordered to attend. Besides, he was too afflicted with pain to compete. However, he changed his mind after listening to Don Cloud.

"What do we have to lose?" Cloud asked. "You'll be in pain wherever you are. This'll be a chance for us to get away for a couple days and we should see guys we haven't seen in a while."

They rode in trucks along the Yalu to Pyoktong. Facilities for track and field events, soccer, American football, baseball, gymnastics, volley ball and so on had been constructed outside the town. Guards were all around, but so were civilians. Then, too, there was food aplenty, although the variety did not change. Everyone acted friendly and cheered all competitors.

Sprouse need not have been concerned about competing. The athletic events were not important, so he had no trouble begging off. Nor did Don Cloud. The mandatory part came at the closing ceremonies, when everyone was assembled for "speeches."

Communist sponsors thanked participants for attending and reminded all that this was a wonderful opportunity to learn about other peoples and cultures. Then it was time for prisoners to speak out. Sergeant Clarence Covington, an NCO of medium height and stocky build, opined benefits went be-

94

yond everyone gathered at Pyoktong. "I believe it's an expression of good friendship for a happier and peaceful tomorrow," he said in closing. With a smirk on his face, the self-assured Covington left the stage.

Corporal Albert Belhomme thought the event "not only benefited us physically and morally but has been a great contribution toward peace." Sergeant D.E. Quarles said, "Our only regret is that the harmonious understanding and peaceful atmosphere experienced here among different races and nations is not yet attained on a world scale."

Ted Sprouse listened squeamishly. The event had portrayed communists as humane, lenient and reasonable, the image they subtly sought to put across. To Sprouse, this did not square with the facts. "Olympians" would return very shortly to the harsh realities of prison camp.

With winter now in full swing, bitterly cold winds swept out of the north. Even though this hut was better constructed than previous ones, it had no means of heating. Nor was there adequate bedding. Prisoners, returning from work details at day's end, were cold soaked. For warmth they bedded down together. "If one turned, we all turned," Sprouse recalled.

Of course, personal clothing never came off. Sprouse would place his overcoat on the floor, while Cloud's was used as a covering blanket. Chills, fevers and flu symptoms were recurrent; yet, everyone eventually recovered. Despite more severe weather conditions than previous winters, all survived—some better than others, of course.

Recurring frostbite inhibited circulation in Sprouse's legs, causing sharp pain and scraping sensations. At its worst, a paralysis crept over his lower extremities and he could not stand nor walk. At one point, he feared he would be shot for malingering.

Again Don Cloud came through, massaging Sprouse's

legs and seeing that he was fed and taken to the latrine. Cloud also covered for Sprouse on work details and protected him from marauding prisoners.

Exacerbating hardships, opportunists continued to plague Camp 4. It was bad enough that progressives were rewarded for cooperating with the enemy, and that they flaunted privileges and influence, but more serious were instances of their disloyalty to fellow Americans.

A colored sergeant—"a good American in every sense of the word," according to Sprouse—suffered such victimization. When he fell ill, he received no comfort whatsoever from captors. Yet Sergeant Covington, suffering similar symptoms, was given medicine and dietary supplements. Covington actually taunted the reactionary as "not deserving" better treatment. When the colored NCO eventually recovered, he "beat the hell out of the Covington" in retribution.

That should have ended the matter; however, Covington "ratted" to headquarters. Within minutes, guards entered the hut with fixed bayonets and ordered the colored sergeant out. He refused, shouting, "Go ahead and bayonet me! Shoot me! But I'm not standing trial for beating up that SOB!" Fearing the man would be killed on the spot, Sprouse interceded, urged the colored the man to go. Ultimately, he did so, stalking out defiantly to take his punishment.

"I probably should not have interfered," Sprouse said upon reflection. "The poor guy would have been better off."

Guards bound the reactionary NCO's hands and feet with wire and tossed him into an abandoned hooch with open doors and windows. There he lay in freezing cold, unable to move. Flesh on his lower limbs actually cracked open in the most vile wounds Sprouse ever saw.

"Upon release, he was out of his mind," according to Sprouse. "He wouldn't talk at all and silently went about do-

96

ing whatever he was told to do. He was just a shell of his former self, thanks to a fellow prisoner's treachery."

Sprouse vowed justice would be served one day, that Covington would be made to pay for this opportunism during the worst of times. Thereafter, Covington was given the "silent treatment" by fellow prisoners. Undeterred, he continued to flaunt his enemy-bestowed favors. Purely and simply, Covington had sold out his comrades and principles to greed.

More perplexing was the case of Richard O. Corden, an opposite of Covington in several respects. Corden stood over six feet tall and was of slender build. Average looking overall, Corden had a pleasant personality and projected a sincere concern for fellow prisoners. "He was well liked by everyone," according to Sprouse.

Deserted by his parents, Corden had been raised by his grandmother, who did her best under austere circumstances. Still Corden had an unhappy childhood. When he matured, he set out to find answers to perceived social problems of the times. This curiosity continued when he entered the Army.

After being captured, he was exposed to Marxism and he was intrigued. He read Marxist classics and everything he could find on socialism. Of course, captors encouraged Corden, gave him time and materials to study, and were always available for discussions. Corden spent his waking hours at headquarters where he studied and wrote critical articles for distribution throughout prison camps.

Yet Corden was principled in his misguided ways. As Sprouse observed: "He stood up to captors when something was unfair, such as a fellow prisoner being abused." Sprouse and Cloud frequently took advantage of Corden to indirectly register complaints against camp authorities. Corden would reflect on the matter, and if he was convinced the point had merit he would openly dispute the communists.

When Sprouse brought up pitfalls of communism, Corden wouldn't be upset. Rather, he would respond with lofty theories of an ideal state. He apparently wanted to analyze all possibilities in his search for "truth." "Although I didn't agree with Corden," Sprouse confessed, "I had to admit he was a decent guy. He was just terribly confused."

The third Christmas in captivity proved memorable. Captors allowed a Christian prayer service led by Sergeant James Richardson. But even this brief respite eventually proved too much for captors. They openly scorned the ritual in progress, and when prisoners prayed "give us this day our daily bread," a guard shouted, "Rubbish! We give you your daily bread!"

"Even when they tried to be lenient," Sprouse noted, "They couldn't pass up a chance to insinuate a message."

At the time, Sprouse was as depressed as he had ever been. With no letters arriving from his wife and family, he assumed they weren't receiving mail either. Incessant communist ranting was getting on his nerves as well.

"What are Americans hearing about us?" he wondered aloud.

"Hang on, Ted," Cloud reminded Sprouse. "Something's going to break soon."

Actually, chances for peace were improving, aided by developments back in the United States. President Dwight D. Eisenhower took office in January 1953, and he promised to end the Korean Conflict. Shortly, he visited the embattled peninsula to back up his commitment. Of course, the United States was but half the equation.

The other half began to come around when Joseph Stalin died in March 1953. With International Communism controlled by Moscow, the Korean Conflict had been Stalin's war from the start. Surely, Stalin's successor would be more reasonable than the "man of steel."

Then, too, the United Nations General Assembly agreed to take up the repatriation issue. Although communists would still take a hard line, the forum offered them a way out of an embarrassing predicament. After Koje-do, UN forces had segregated communist prisoners into those who wished to be repatriated and those who wished to remain in the free world. When half refused to return, the outcome was not acceptable to communists who charged prisoners had been coerced by interrogators.

Despite continued intractability, communists allowed a limited exchange of sick and wounded in 1953. In Operation Little Switch at the end of April, 6,670 communist prisoners were exchanged for 684 UN prisoners. The first tentative step toward an armistice had been taken.

It seemed to Sprouse that several Americans released under Little Switch were not particularly debilitated—and they were known progressives. But that was to be expected, since communists determined who would be freed. That some initial returnees would say favorable things about captors surely figured into the calculation.

But true patriots had been released, too. As proof, within a week UN planes flew over and bombed a nearby supply dump. Those just released had pinpointed the target for debriefers and the air force followed up. As prisoners cheered and waved to let pilots know they had scored well, the planes went into victory rolls and roared away.

"Why do you applaud?" an angry interpreter demanded. "Your very own planes were trying to bomb you and missed. Your government is upset because you have not cooperated with peace-loving peoples of the world. You are a disgrace to mankind and won't be released any time soon!"

Prisoners scoffed at first. What idiocy! At that point, they were sanguine about their own chances for early release, but as weeks passed with no more news they began to wonder.

Communists were still wrestling with paranoia. They remained suspicious of the International Red Cross; however, they did trust neutral nations, all of whom were more or less revolutionists. So it was through a plan advanced by India that peace would come to Korea that summer.

Of course, prisoners had only an inkling of what was transpiring. Sprouse and Cloud discussed letters being circulated for signature, but both dismissed them as another propaganda ruse. However, some letters reached intended destinations. A typical letter follows:

To: Representatives of all countries
POW Camp in the United Nations
Democratic People's General Assembly
Republic of Korea

February 22, 1953

Dear Sirs:

We, the under signed, have been prisoners of war over two years. During this two years our welfare has never been neglected and our stay here has been made as comfortable as possible. But personal comfort can never substitute the yearning which we all have to return to our families and our natural desire to return home still remains in spite of the fact we are being treated well and living comfortably.

We have been closely following the Korean Armistice Negotiations with the hope that these negotiations would arrive at a successful settlement of the Korean question, but so far our hopes and desires have not been realized.

Since the repatriation of POWs is to be discussed during the seventh session of the General Assembly to be held February this year, we wish to appeal to all the members of the General Assembly to do everything within your power to settle the issue on the repatriation of prisoners as soon as possible so that we may return to our homes in the shortest possible time.

We think that the only possible way of settling this issue is to cease hostilities immediately and adhere to the practice of International Law and the Geneva Convention on the total repatriation of prisoners of war, only in this way can our hopes and desires of returning be fulfilled.

We remain,
truly yours

A long list of signatures followed.

Although dithering continued, the communists eventually agreed to a Neutral Nation Repatriation Commission that would validate prisoners' choices. The drawn-out interviews finally were completed in June. Even though more than half their prisoners still refused repatriation, communists accepted results this time.

Then they dropped a bombshell!

Twenty-one Americans, one British, and 315 Republic of Korea soldiers had decided to remain behind the Bamboo Curtain. Despite the huge difference in totals, the world was stunned by the news that any American—even a turncoat!—would refuse freedom.

Richard Corden was one of the twenty-one Americans. To the very end Sprouse urged Corden to reconsider, suggesting that he could more objectively ponder merits of Marxism in an open society. But Corden politely refused. Sprouse concluded fear of retribution for progressive activities had now been added to early life trauma and pseudo-intellectualism to overwhelm Corden. (As a footnote, in 1958 Richard Corden requested repatriation back to the United States. Altogether, sixteen of the original twenty-one returned, one died in China, one went to Czechoslovakia, one to Poland and two remained.)

Abruptly, it seemed, belligerents signed an armistice on July 27, 1953. The good news was that most American prisoners in North Korea at long last would be released. The bad news was that anxious moments still awaited Ted Sprouse and Don Cloud as they continued to endure the torturous rituals of communist diplomacy.

IX
COMING HOME

Americans at home and abroad wanted prisoners of war released immediately. And why not! Hadn't an armistice been signed! Hadn't the war stopped! Nonetheless, suspense continued a while longer—for several reasons.

First, there was paranoia. Totalitarian states such as China and Korea considered all institutions tools of government. Even humane and charitable agencies had to fall in line. More to the point, they believed all states were the same in this respect. Thus, communists would not accept "outside" help in a prisoner exchange. Then, too, Little Switch had set a precedent when it was carried off by military from both sides.

Yet, the International Red Cross insisted on a role in Big Switch, the exchange of remaining prisoners. To overcome opposition, the Red Cross formed Joint Teams that would visit camps without delay. The combination worked well enough in UN camps but not in the north. China's Red Crossers were more intent on finding fault with their counterparts than with conditions in North Korean prison camps. Also, a lack of interpreters hampered coordinating visits; consequently, most North Korean camps were emptied before Joint Teams arrived.

Next, Marxists regarded this as just another battle in a worldwide struggle, so they pushed for concessions and a propaganda edge in Korea. As a result, negotiations were anything but expedient.

Then there was South Korean President Syngman Rhee who wanted Korea united under his government. Rhee even released some North Koreans ahead of time to undercut negotiations. Although Rhee was brought into line eventually, his antics caused delays.

Finally, there was a shortage of transportation. North Korea's primitive modes had been all but destroyed during the war, so evacuating 13,000 UN prisoners would be time-consuming under the best of conditions. As matters stood, conditions were anything but ideal.

Of course, prisoners bore the brunt of disharmony and delays. Ted Sprouse and Don Cloud were encouraged when the quality and quantity of food improved in early summer. But their hopes had been dashed too many times before to be optimistic now. Near the end of July, however, hopes shot to new highs when a UN fighter plane flew in low one evening, buzzed the camp several times, dipped its wings and went into victory rolls as it flew away.

Everyone rushed outside to wave and shout in response. Clearly, the pilot had been telling them something. But what? Perhaps in the morning they would be told.

Doubts returned when guards at roll call were as surly and arrogant as ever. They appeared to know of nothing new. Then, almost routinely, the following day an interpreter announced an armistice and that prisoners would be going home soon. No schedule, though, other than sick and wounded would leave first.

Operation Big Switch actually began on August 5th, 1953, with 400 UN prisoners of war passing southward through the demarcation zone. At the same time, 2800 communist prisoners were passing through going the other way. The prisoners to be released on any given day were selected by respective belligerents, of course. The operation was drawn out because of the logistics involved in handling the large numbers of prisoners with an inadequate system.

Halfway through August, the NCOs in Camp 4 crowded

onto trucks for transhipment south. Heavy rains caused delays, as roaring waters cut deep trenches in mountain roads and swept away bridges. Huddling rain-soaked prisoners often sat on trucks hours at a time while Koreans scrambled to patch roadways. Prisoner patience wore out when the convoy came upon a washed-out bridge ten miles short of the rail station. They volunteered to walk the rest of the way—gladly! This time guards accommodated prisoners, although somewhat reluctantly.

At the railhead, NCOs crowded into boxcars as animals would—but "happy animals" they were. For three days they journeyed southward in anything but comfortable circumstances. Then they loaded onto trucks for the next stretch.

Sprouse had no idea of the route taken and he didn't ask. Even if guards knew they weren't likely to answer directly or honestly. The important thing now was that Ted Sprouse was going home; coarse treatment and primitive facilities mattered little with the end in sight.

Eventually, they reached Tent City at Kaesong, where Sprouse would spend another twelve days in captivity. Cloud was assigned to a different tent, the first time he and Sprouse had been separated since August 1950. After settling in, however, they met outside and gazed at a big balloon floating over the demarcation zone. Beyond that balloon was freedom!

Even in Tent City, Korean guards manned machine guns to keep prisoners under control. When Sprouse asked who would be fool enough to take a chance now, Cloud thought a bit and said, "Some habits are hard to break, I guess."

They ran into several old acquaintances in Tent City, some given up as dead long ago. But all had prevailed and now stood happily at freedom's door. One in particular stood apart.

105

The prisoner who had gone crazy early on was now functioning normally. For thirty months he had carried off a grand deception. When Sprouse expressed surprise upon seeing him, the "looney" smiled and said, "Fooled you, too, huh? Well, it was worth it! They thought I was nuts so they left me alone. No brainwashing, no dark holes, nuthin'."

"Lucky you weren't shot," Sprouse countered.

"But then we all were," was the response.

For some, Tent City was not carefree. Since only sixty names daily were called for exchange, the remainder were disappointed. One day a GI snapped when the last name had been called and his was not included. Faced with at least one more night behind barbed wire, the poor guy rushed the nearest guard. He veered away at the last instant, ducked and ran headlong into a telephone pole. He panicked when he noted blood now running down his face.

Sprouse grabbed a blanket, soaked it in water and, helped by others, wrapped the flailing prisoner in a makeshift strait jacket. Once subdued, he settled down and lived to be released a couple days later.

Ted Sprouse received his first Red Cross parcel in Tent City. His initial reaction was to ask, "Why now?" Food supplements, health aids and toiletries would have been the difference between death and survival for many in prison camps. But now prisoners had everything they needed—and more!

Of course, Sprouse was unaware that the Red Cross had been stymied at every turn during the war. Nor was he aware— nor likely to be appreciative—of what the organization had done for thousands of Chinese and Korean prisoners who had declined repatriation to their homelands. Thus, Sprouse and other ex-prisoners were inclined to disparage the belated packet as too little, too late. It was an understandable conclusion, albeit an unfair one for the Red Cross.

On the eleventh day in Tent City, Sprouse's name was called for the five-mile trip to Panmunjom. When Cloud's name was not called—they would not cross to freedom together!—Ted decided to ask for a delay. But Cloud wouldn't hear of it.

"The important thing is we made it, Ted," Cloud reminded his friend. "You go and I'll see you over there tomorrow."

On that last night in captivity, Ted Sprouse shaved away the heavy growth of whiskers. He regretted not being able to take a snapshot of his unkempt appearance—as if he would need a reminder! He smiled as he mused aloud, "Now they won't call me 'Pop' anymore."

His mind racing with expectations for the morrow, Ted slept very little that night. Then at last the day he had yearned for so long arrived. Ted Sprouse was freed September 2, 1953, having spent thirty-three months to the day in captivity. The date was also little Steve's third birthday. What poetic coincidences!

Ted was the last man to mount the truck, so he was the first off "on the other side." As his feet touched ground, a Chinese guard tumbled off the truck to sprawl ingloriously in dirt nearby. The perpetrator of this mischief was the GI who had lost his wedding band—and finger!—that first day of capture so long ago. The avenging GI just couldn't resist punching out one more "gook" upon departing North Korea.

A general greeted Ted with a handshake, saying, "Welcome home, son!"

The second person he encountered was Gordon Gammack of the *Des Moines Register and Tribune.* Before Ted could answer Gammack's first question, however, an American lieutenant cautioned Sprouse not to say anything that might jeopardize those not yet released.

"Don't worry, Lieutenant," Sprouse replied. "The best friend I'll ever have is still over there."

Sprouse enjoyed his first hot shower in 1008 days. Afterwards, he dusted with DDT to finally rid himself of vermin before putting on brand-new underwear and uniform. The noon meal included roast beef, mashed potatoes and gravy—all unseasoned. There was ice cream, too. Vanilla ice cream! Ted Sprouse ate mostly ice cream to soothe an excited stomach.

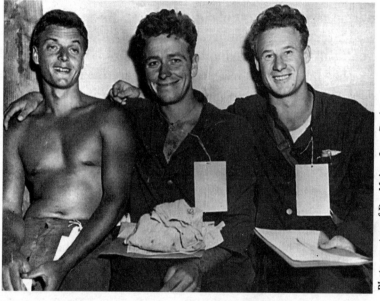

Photo courtesy of Des Moines Iowa Register.

Photo appearing in The Des Moines Register. Left to right: Cpl Donald R. Bittner, Pittsburgh, PA, SFC Ted R. Sprouse, Drakesville, IA, and SFC Arlo L. Robb, Unioniville, IA. Photo appearing in the Iowa newspaper had Cpl. Bittner cropped out. Original caption read, South of Inchon, at Freedom Village, Sgts Sprouse and Robb beam with joy after their repatriation.

After lunch, Sprouse joined others for the twenty-minute helicopter ride to a processing station. There a clerk helped him put together a brief of Ted's time in captivity. Sprouse described woundings and injuries he had suffered, provided dates of capture and release, and gave names, approximate dates and locations of those he had helped bury. He did not mention incidents of disloyalty among prisoners; Ted believed he needed more time to mull that one over.

He now learned he had been promoted to tech sergeant while in prison camp. It was a fair step, for Sprouse had been performing duties of the higher rank while in combat. Promotion pay, plus the accrued ten dollars a month he had allowed himself, now added up to more than $900. Of course, Joanne had been receiving most of his pay all along. Ted took $100 for spending money; the rest he would draw out when he was separated from service back in the states.

At the post exchange, Ted bought cigarettes and toilet articles. Mostly, he looked around, incredulous of the affluence he beheld. He also kept an eye out for Don Cloud, who could show up any time now. Ted asked everyone he bumped into about Cloud, but no one had seen him here in South Korea.

Ex-prisoners were housed apart. Lights were left burning all night long, lest prisoners wake up in darkness and conclude they were still in captivity. Ted spent that first night of freedom on a soft mattress; rather, he intended to. When the charge of quarters entered the ward the next morning, he found Sprouse and others sleeping on the floor—beds were too soft!

On September 2nd in Centerville, Iowa, Joanne received official notification that Ted had returned to "military control in Korea." The next day she received a second telegram:

When Sprouse entrucked for Inchon to board the USS *Brewster*, he still hadn't heard from Don Cloud. However, he had been assured that American prisoners were still being released on schedule. Somewhat relieved, Ted concluded they probably would link up in San Francisco.

109

=MA025 SSJ040   1953 SEP 2 AM 9 09

M.OTA037 XV GOVT PDWUX WASHINGTON DC VIA CENTERVILLE IOWA
=MRS JOANNE D SPROUSE, DLR IMMY

THE SECRETARY OF THE ARMY HAS ASKED ME TO INFORM YOU THAT
YOUR HUSBAND SFC SPROUSE TEDDY R. WAS RETURNED TO MILITARY
CONTROL IN KOREA AND WILL BE RETURNED TO THE UNITED STATES
BY SURFACE TRANSPORTATION AT AN EARLY DATE. YOU WILL BE
ADVISED OF ARRIVAL DATE=
     =WM E BERGIN MAJOR GENERAL USA THE ADJUTANT GENERAL
     OF THE ARMY=

MA165 SSA725

M.OTA186 67 3 EXTRA COLLECT 1.43 XF TOKYO VIA RCA
VIA CENTERVILLE IOWA 3=   1953 SEP 3 PM 5
LT MRS TED SPROUSE=
     CARE JACK THOMPSON FONE 7597-M=BURLINGTON IOWA=

DEAREST JOANNE FREED FROM THE REDS   AT LAST THANKS BE TO
GOD ALIVE AND WELL RECEIVING EXCELLENT CARE   ONE LOOK AT
YOU AND ILL BE OK ON MY   HOME BY BOAT TELL THE FOLKS
LOVE TO ALL AT HOME ALL MY LOVE DEAREST=
     TED

Telegrams upon Sprouse's release, September 1953.

110

Throughout the voyage home, ex-prisoners were separated from other troops. They were served special diets for one thing. Then they were interviewed several times by doctors and psychiatrists. An hour of news reels was shown each day to bring prisoners up to date on current events. Although these sessions were voluntary, Ted attended every one. Often he was startled at what he saw and heard—Americans, including reporters, knew so little about communists.

Intelligence specialists interviewed NCOs. Basically, interviewers were interested in communist methods in dealing with prisoners. Surely, tips from those who had endured brainwashing would be helpful as the Cold War continued unabated. Sergeant Sprouse described Chinese "lenient" treatment in scathing terms. Although he had already mellowed somewhat, Ted could not rid himself of the notion that reds were "animals"—and incorrigibly so!

An Inspector General asked Sprouse about anyone who might deserve punishment. Ted recoiled from harsh judgments, but he was forthright when Sergeant Covington's name came up. Besides mentioning the subject's unprofessionalism, Sprouse described Covington's "ratting" on the colored sergeant and the consequences thereof. But even here, Ted was cautious.

"I just know what I saw with my own eyes," he said. "Better talk to other prisoners before you draw conclusions."

"You'll probably hear more on this in months to come," the investigator concluded.

The *Brewster* docked in San Francisco at daybreak on September 21st, 1953. Ex-prisoners were all on deck—they wouldn't have missed this view for anything! Ted Sprouse, resplendent in a freshly pressed uniform with tech sergeant's stripes affixed, was among them. He watched a brightly colored boat circle below, broadcasting lively music and displaying a huge "Welcome Home!" sign. People at dockside waved and called out. The scene was everything Sprouse thought it would be.

Another boat pulled alongside with "brass" on board. Shortly, mail was delivered. Sprouse was handed a packet of letters, many times the number he had received while a prisoner. With shaking hands, Ted opened a letter from his wife. Tears blurred his vision as he read sentence after shocking sentence. When he finished, he carefully folded the letter and set it aside.

"She's found somebody else," he muttered aloud.

Considering the emotional trash pile his life had become, Ted was not surprised. He yearned to talk to Don Cloud. Stoically, Sprouse approached the nearest clerk and asked if Cloud had arrived. The clerk checked passenger lists before saying, "No, he hasn't."

"I want the fastest way home," Ted demanded. "How can I do that?"

"We'll book you on a flight later today," the clerk promised.

When he entered the reception center ashore, Sprouse heard his name being called over a public address system. He was told to report to the Red Cross desk. A smiling young lady in Red Cross uniform handed Ted a phone and announced, "It's your mother."

"Mom?"

"Yes, Ted. It's me!"

After that, the conversation blurred. Ted spoke a few words to his mother, father, brothers and sisters before promising to see them all in Des Moines tomorrow.

To while away remaining hours before catching his flight, Ted went to the NCO Club. Volunteers had gathered there to entertain returning prisoners. Later, a nurse from Mason City,

Iowa, drove Sprouse and Richard Collet of Ottumwa on a tour of picturesque San Francisco. Ted turned down all drink offers, fearing he couldn't tolerate alcohol after so long an abstinence.

At the airport for an eight p.m. flight, Ted learned he would be delayed because of the plane's malfunctioning engine. Two hours later, the problem had been solved and the plane departed. In Denver, Ted learned he had missed the connecting flight to Des Moines, so he was booked on another through Omaha. Time passed quickly during the holdover, for Ted talked with ex-prisoners he probably would never see again.

Sprouse flew from Omaha to Des Moines with Collet and his sailor brother, who was on liberty for the occasion. As they neared Des Moines, a stewardess asked them to leave last to avoid congestion on the tarmac.

"Your families are waiting," she explained. "There'll be quite a celebration."

As the plane taxied to the Des Moines terminal at mid-morning, Ted glimpsed loved ones gathered there. Benumbed, he walked off the plane and into the arms of his mother at the foot of the steps. Then he hugged his father. He went down the line: Don, Betty, Lois, Shirley, Kyle, Mary Jane and Karen. Glancing up, he spotted his wife standing silently apart and holding the hand of a toddler. Little Steve!

Shirley choked back a sob. Ted was terribly thin and he walked with a slight limp. Even after three weeks of rest and nourishment, her formerly robust brother probably weighed no more than 130 pounds—down from 180!

When initial excitement had subsided, Don drew Ted aside, and said, "There's something I got to tell you."

"I think I know what it is," Ted replied. "It can wait."

The trip to Drakesville was a rarity in quiet Iowa coun-

113

tryside. Family and friends drove in tandem to Ottumwa where they joined a waiting caravan. Then the parade continued down the highway with blaring horns, flapping banners and boisterous cheers. Unabashedly, Ted Sprouse was being welcomed back from his odyssey. He had come home, indeed!

X
PROBING THE DEPTHS

"It was not a good idea," Shirley Sprouse MacDonald concluded years later. She was speaking of the crowd at the airport, the long caravan to Drakesville and the colorful Bloomfield ceremony when Ted was presented a key to the city. "We should have just let Ted settle in, let him adjust at his own pace."

Everyone, especially proud father Charlie, had thought the spectacle would convince Ted—and everyone else!—that he was universally welcomed and supported. Besides, keeping busy wouldn't allow him time to think about the mess he was coming home to, would it?

Ted posed with Joanne, Steve and family members for cameramen and answered reporters' questions with courteous and heroic demeanor, but he was overwhelmed. There

Ted receives the Key to the City of Bloomfield in 1953 from Mayor Arthur Stookesberry.

Welcome Home parade in Drakesville, Iowa.

was irony, too, for inwardly he felt rejected by the one he had been counting on the most through long and desolate months. Just beneath the outward calm, anger seethed.

Back at the house in Drakesville that evening, Don told Ted there were things he should know about Joanne right away. Again Ted cut short the discussion, telling his brother, "I want to hear it from her."

When Joanne said she preferred to return to her house that first night, Don, who lived in Centerville at the time, drove them to the place she had rented in the country. After being dropped off, Ted got to the point.

"Joanne, tell me what's going on," he began. "You said in a letter there was somebody else, and Don has been trying to tell me something. I need the truth."

Joanne dismissed any behavioral lapses as trivial. She admitted going out with other men, but insisted "no one knew." She had been discreet. Her tone throughout suggested she and Ted could work things out, if he would just be reasonable. But Ted questioned her sincerity. She seemed manipu-

116

lative, self serving. He was becoming ever more suspicious of this "stranger" as she continued talking.

Ted learned many things that night. Joanne had had a baby back in August, just weeks before he returned! She had rented this house in the country and had furnished it for her and Steve. And there was no money left from the allotments she had received for three years. Overall, she seemed unrepentant, unconcerned about infidelity.

For the second night in a row Ted went without sleep. Joanne had gone to bed in the wee hours—by herself. Ted spent the night in the living room, smoking and thinking. He was crushed emotionally—and terribly confused.

Even his meeting with little Steve had been subdued. After all, the toddler was puzzled by this "new man in his life." Steve was more at home with Grandpa and Grandma, Mr. and Mrs. Clem Anderson, who had been raising him. Well, Ted resolved to win Steve over eventually—doing whatever would be necessary to reclaim lost time.

Ted Sprouse meets his son, Stephen Sprouse, 3, for the first time. Others in the picture are Ted's mother, Joanne and his father.

Photo by Des Moines Tribune

In the meantime, he had to decide on Joanne. When she got up, Ted told her they would all return to Drakesville for a few days. When she started to protest, he cut her off.

"I know it won't be pleasant for you," he acknowledged, "but I want you to suffer. And if you have a conscience at all, you'll be miserable!"

Don, expecting his brother would want out of the arrangement when he learned the facts, drove up at that point. Don appeared relieved when he saw Ted's family up and about; perhaps, he had feared violence may have occurred. Don also seemed relieved when Ted asked for a ride back to Drakesville.

Ida May was polite and considerate, even though she was torn by her son's torment. She called Ted aside out in the yard one evening, took his hand, looked him in the eye and said, "I don't know what you'll do. I wish I could tell you what to do, but I just don't know. You've got to work it out with Joanne or leave her, but don't go on as you are. If you want to stay married to Joanne, I'll treat her the same as the rest of my daughters. I'll do my best to accept her."

"I'm not sure you can do that, Mom," Ted replied. "Do you really know what she did to me? Do you know she had a baby while I was gone? Put it up for adoption with me as the father? Do you know she spent money I was sending to pay her boyfriend's drunken driving fine?"

He paused to let his mother think about those things, but she surprised him by saying, "Everyone knows, Ted."

Ted saw hurt in his mother's face—deep, deep hurt. She had been suffering with this for a long, long time. It occurred to Ted that this was worse than Rex's death in at least one respect: Nothing could be done about Rex so she had come to terms with his loss. But in Ted's case, the pain was ongoing and would end only after he reconciled himself to the inevitable choice he must make.

Upon reflecting on all that his mother had been through—losing a brother in World War I, losing a son in World War II, and enduring his own long imprisonment—Ted's self-absorption ended.

"I'll do the right thing," he said softly. Together, they walked into the family house.

In time remaining on his convalescent leave, Ted worked it out. He could never abide betrayal; he had seen too much of that in North Korea. Thus, he could never bring himself to be caring about Joanne again. What kind of life would that be?

So, he returned Joanne and Steve to Centerville and hired a lawyer. With Ida May often accompanying him, he roamed through southeast Iowa putting his case together. He had become reconciled to the fate he had returned to—so it seemed. He would divorce his wife and settle for visitations with Steve. Doggedly, he worked with the lawyer and was awarded a divorce decree in late November 1953.

In the meantime, he still had unfinished business with the Army. So Ted drove his new Olds-88 Super to Fort Sheridan, Illinois, in late October. Before he could be discharged, however, his official records had to be completed. That initial session upon being freed had been a makeshift approach to get him paid and off on convalescent leave. Now he had to satisfy all legal and regulatory requirements.

Ted did his best to recall what had transpired in prison camp. A health record would be crucial, for Ted was daily reminded that he was far from healthy again. He learned the army did not grant disability compensation: that would have to come from the Veterans Administration.

During processing, Ted met three other sergeants—"Ash" Ashpole, Nick Nakkuori and "Pollock" Poloski—who also had been prisoners. The foursome spent a lot of time together, usually gathering at the NCO Club. Given the circumstances, they tended to be a bit unruly—even disrespectful of authority. Several times they were reprimanded; thus, their discharges on October 28, 1953, came as a relief at the separation center.

Afterwards, Ted and his friends headed for Milwaukee, Nick's home. The reunion of these men who understood one another continued for several more days. Then almost on impulse Ted announced he had to return to Iowa; he had celebrated long enough.

His next stop was the Dubuque packing plant, where his father was in charge of sheep shearing. Charlie was highly pleased that Ted had dropped by. He proudly took Ted to meet the boss and co-workers. His father's glowing accounts not only embarrassed Ted but annoyed him as well. "He has no idea how inglorious it all was," Ted thought to himself.

Upon noting his son's discomfiture, Charlie stopped bragging and somewhat apologetically asked, "What can I do for you, Ted?"

"I need a job."

"Sure, I'll take it up with the front office."

"I mean today, this afternoon," Ted insisted.

Charlie hustled away and returned to announce Ted was hired. So he went to work that very day. Wrestling with resisting lambs strained his back and legs, but he persisted. When others commented on how quickly he got back in form, Ted ignored the remarks. "It's nothing compared to carrying logs with a broken back and on a starvation diet," he mused to himself. He had just about given up convincing people that POW prison camps were not prideful experiences. With one exception, he kept those thoughts to himself, however.

Ted Sprouse shearing sheep in April 1954, eight months after his release from the POW camp. He would win first place at the Iowa State Fair two years later.

Don Cloud called in early November, desperately needing to talk to Ted. Arrangements were made and Cloud, still in the Army and stationed at Huntsville, Alabama, took leave and headed for Drakesville. Upon seeing his friend again, Ted noted telltale signs. After meeting and exchanging pleasantries with Ted's family, he and Cloud headed for a Bloomfield bar.

"I was glad to hear you made it out," Ted announced when they were seated. "I was beginning to wonder what happened."

Cloud explained that he followed a day or two behind Sprouse, usually just missing him at the processing centers. "I made a pest out of myself inquiring, believe me." he said.

With a beer in hand, they proceeded to bring each other up to date. Cloud listened attentively as Ted told about his marital problems upon returning. Don agreed that Ted had no choice but to divorce Joanne and go on from there.

"It would have been tough any time," Cloud mused. "In your frame of mind, not a chance." Following up on the thought, he continued, "Ted, you're the only one I can talk to. I wish we lived closer so we could get together once in a while. That would help preserve our sanity."

"But at least your marriage is solid," Ted reminded him.

"I'll just say we're getting by," was the reply. "And

Don Cloud and his wife "Freddie" in early 1954. (Cloud was with Ted Sprouse throughout his prison ordeal)

The Sprouse family celebrates Christmas, 1953. Back row: Shirley, Betty, Kyle, Ray and Mary Jane. Front row: Mom, Ted, Lois, Dad and Karen.

it's not my wife Freddie's fault most of the time. She's fighting like hell to hold our marriage together."

"A divorce is a terrible thing, Don. As long as she's faithful to you, I'd sure try to make it work."

They talked of many other things, but the visit was foreshortened. Cloud couldn't stay overnight because of "family matters" that had to be taken care of. Sprouse didn't press Cloud to change his plans; he knew his friend too well to try that. They embraced upon departing and vowed to meet again soon.

Sprouse went back to shearing sheep and trying to make sense of his life. A bright spot was little Steve. According to the divorce ruling, Ted would have Steve half the time between January and June and for summer vacations.

Ted regularly drove to Centerville to pick up Steve at Grandma Anderson's and bring him to Drakesville. Charlie and Ida May loved their grandson and looked forward to his visits. Steve would sleep with his father and spend days with his grandmother while Ted worked. Heartbreak time inevita-

123

bly came when Steve had to return to Centerville. Ted got along well with the Andersons, but he thought it strange that Joanne was seldom there—nor did she ever inquire about Steve while he was at the Sprouses.

Baseball, the other big activity in Ted Sprouse's life, was no longer possible. He tried catching a game the first summer back with a pick-up team but quit after a couple innings. His back, legs and feet wouldn't let him react readily or quickly. Pain and poor circulation had taken away his mobility afoot. True, he had regained his normal weight and much of his former strength, but overall he had lost the competitive edge that had made him exceptional in the past.

Then there was desire. His perspective had changed: Playing a game seemed not all that important anymore. When urged to try again, Ted would dismiss the suggestion with "I have nothing to prove now." The dream—to play professional baseball—had evaporated during his sojourn in North Korea.

On occasion, Ted would attend a game in Drakesville. Always he would be noted by fans who remembered his glory days behind the plate in those parts. He appreciated the fans' loyalty but dismissed flattering remarks as gratuitous. He didn't need sympathy or accommodation.

He was asked to umpire games. Since he had spent a lot of time looking at balls and strikes from a catcher's perspective, he undoubtedly could call a respectable game. But having loved playing so much, Ted couldn't bring himself to settle for umpiring. At least not yet.

During free time, Ted frequently drove to Bloomfield where Shirley and Mary Jane now lived. Shirley worked for Whitacre Cleaners and Mary for Davis County State Bank. After the girls finished for the day, the threesome would go on an outing or to supper. Ted enjoyed his sisters' company; they were lighthearted and upbeat conversationalists and he needed such stimuli. One evening, however, the occasion ended awkwardly.

They had gone to a cafe after golfing. When Shirley mentioned the food was not tasty, Ted cut her off, saying, "Until you've eaten wormy corn you don't know what tasty food is." The remark embarrassed the girls to silence.

Adding to discomfiture, the jukebox began playing *Vaya Con Dios*, a vintage tune by Les Paul and Mary Ford. As the hauntingly sentimental song continued, Ted stood up and gritted, "Let's get out of here!" The Sprouse sisters had glimpsed the emotional turmoil churning inside their brother.

Ted traded his still-new car for an Olds-88 Convertible. If he was to live the high life, he would do so in style! Night after night he drove to various hotspots and returned home intoxicated. Sometimes he called Don Cloud after a binge and the two would commiserate at length.

Sprouse family members avoided Ted at such times. They felt his pain but puzzled over what to do about it. Because they worked together, Charlie frequently suffered embarrassment. For example, Ted would shear one more lamb than his father just to show up the "old man."

Sundays were especially tense. Ted was sloughing off his vow to serve God after surviving—and he felt guilty as hell! When he saw others going to church services, Ted would become unbearable to anyone around. In a perverse way, religion, too, had become a target of Ted Sprouse's bitterness.

At his mother's suggestion—and because he was passing blood and vomiting regularly—Ted entered the Veterans Administration hospital in Des Moines. He told doctors he was at loose ends, that he couldn't work and needed disability compensation to order to get by. Ted was turned over to counselors, whom he regarded as naive and simplistic. What could they possibly know about disorders resulting from communist prison camps?

One counselor confronted Ted, telling him to stop feeling sorry for himself. "If you'd done your duty, you would have escaped or would have been killed trying," the doctor said. That statement ended rapport with Ted Sprouse, of course.

Treatment of other disorders was more successful, however. Through medicine and diet, Ted's stomach became less troublesome. Whirlpools and massages relaxed tissues and improved circulation in his legs. Ted left the hospital feeling better. Six months later he was granted a ten percent disability rating, which translated into a modest check each month. Thus fortified, he returned to shearing sheep, drinking beer and getting along with family and friends.

A year after the visit of Don Cloud, Ted bumped into someone who was to turn his life around. It was at Carrie's Tavern in Bloomfield that he heard a familiar voice. Looking up, Ted saw Eloise Brunk, niece of proprietor Willis Kratzer. Eloise wasn't there to drink; she had come to see her uncle.

They struck up a conversation—Eloise over a soda and Ted over a beer—and learned they had known each other in younger days. They updated each other on changes since they last talked. Eloise was aware of Ted's prisoner-of-war escapades, having followed his return in news accounts. They exchanged phone numbers and he called the next day. Although Ted drank a little too much to suit her, Eloise rationalized that was because of trauma he had suffered. She, too, had taken a few lumps over the years.

Eloise had been raised by her grandparents, so Uncle Willis was like a brother to her. She had rushed into marriage at sixteen but divorced an abusive husband after eight years. She then set out to make a living for herself and three-year-old daughter Vicki, which Eloise was doing handily enough. Upon seeing Ted again, things changed. She had met a kindred soul.

126

As for Ted, he found Eloise strikingly pretty. She dressed neatly and conversed openly and readily. The more he talked to her, the more he realized she was energetic and intelligent. Most important, he found her to be a mature listener.

With much in common, Ted and Eloise began spending most of their free time together.

Ted usually kept her informed on his work routine and daily plans, but he didn't tell her about a trip to Des Moines that fall. Quite naturally, Eloise wondered what Ted was up to when he left without explaining.

Sprouse had been summoned by an Army criminal investigator working on the Sergeant Covington case. Since the matter was sensitive, Ted had been instructed to tell no one. Until public announcements were eventually made of the POW-camp investigations, Eloise had to be kept in the dark. Thus, the first snag occurred in their budding romance.

At Federal Building in Des Moines, Ted was questioned under oath in a follow up of earlier statements. He was told that charges were being preferred against Covington, a development Sprouse viewed as only just. Sprouse was sent home and told to be available for possible appearance as a court witness. Again he was admonished to keep all this confidential.

Eloise felt slighted when Ted returned and acted as though nothing had happened. Noting her pique, Ted reminded her of a timeless truth: "If you don't trust me now, Eloise, you'll never trust me. In that case, we have no future together."

She accepted this bit of wisdom and the courtship continued. This minor crisis had been the last hurdle, for Ted and Eloise married on December 11, 1954. A seemingly short courtship and hasty marriage proved timely for both. Forty-three years later Ted reflected on the event: "If I hadn't found Eloise when I did, I wouldn't be here today. She showed a lot

Wedding photo of Ted Sprouse and Eloise Brunk, December 11, 1954.

of patience, a lot of tolerance."

As a footnote, Sprouse was not called to actually testify at Sergeant Covington's court-martial; however, Ted's statements were used to help convict Covington. He was found guilty and sentenced to thirty years at hard labor in Fort Leavenworth, Kansas.

Ted and Eloise bought a home in Bloomfield and furnished it modestly. Three months later, Ted switched from beer to soft drinks. Then he entered counseling under a more receptive psychiatrist at Veterans Hospital. Therapy consisted of Ted's opening up, confronting the trauma that was making him irrational at times and miserable most of the time. The therapist urged Ted to write an account of those stark prison days and nights. Laboriously, Ted did so, and ever so slowly the gloom lifted, no doubt facilitated by the birth of Rodney on May 18, 1956.

In spite of chronic back pain, Ted continued shearing sheep. He won first place at the Iowa State Fair in 1956, shearing four lambs in a little over four minutes. Although he was encouraged by such accomplishments, Sprouse's burdensome rehabilitation had not run full course by any means.

He went to work at the Bloomfield Post Office as a letter carrier in 1957. He now had to walk a lot, but Ted handled the job readily. Certainly, it was less strenuous than shearing sheep. He got along well with fellow workers and enjoyed meeting and greeting people on his route. He was recognized as the POW-camp survivor, a status that impressed most Bloomfielders.

For a while, things went well for the Sprouses. Ted earned enough to support his family, and a regular work schedule allowed time for a garden and the children's activities. He loved Vicki as much as he would have loved his own daughter. Ted was immensely proud of her achievements in school and community events. Even though Rodney was but a youngster, Ted started grooming him for baseball by teaching him to throw and catch and swing a bat. And there were Steve's visitations.

Since Steve was attending school, he could only visit Ted and Eloise on holidays and during summer vacations. Steve now lived with his mother and her second husband near

Ottumwa, some twenty miles to the north. Vicki and Rodney loved their big brother because he taught them games and fun things to do. Of note, Ted and Eloise never brought up the divorce and Steve's "other family." Although he and Eloise wished Steve didn't have to shuttle back and forth, they were satisfied this arrangement was the best they could make under the circumstances.

Ted's behavior on Sundays continued to be worrisome, however. He kept himself under control for the most part, but there were outbursts. One Sunday he picked up the plate of chicken Eloise had prepared for dinner and dashed it to the floor. Eloise rushed to salvage the meal while Vicki and Rodney scampered away terrified.

"Leave it alone!" Ted shouted. Then he composed himself and said, "I made the mess, I'll clean it up."

Then there was the uniform episode at the post office. Ted would go to Ottumwa to buy uniforms, a practice that did not sit well with his boss. When Ted was accused of being disloyal to Bloomfield merchants, it was a charge Ted wouldn't tolerate. If he was considered disloyal, there was only one thing to do. He quit!

After that display of temper, Ted did two things: He returned to shearing sheep and he sought out God. Eloise supported him and together they went looking for a church. With definite ideas about religion, Ted wasn't easy to satisfy. As they attended various services and talked to various pastors, Ted saw merits—but he also saw deficiencies. So the search went on.

At a friend's suggestion, they drove ten miles west to attend Mark Baptist Church. Ted liked what he saw and heard, for the pastor was straightforward with a clear message: The Lord Jesus Christ was the Savior and had died for all mankind's sins. Ted listened and for the first time since he had prayed in the ditch he was at peace. He and Eloise became regular worshippers there in 1961.

Thereafter, Sundays were more peaceful and pleasant at the Ted Sprouse home. Ted had rid himself of guilt by fulfilling the pledge he had made a decade earlier on a cold and chaotic night.

For the next couple years, life for the Sprouses flowed contentedly. But in 1964 a series of health crises turned everything upside down. First, Ted's mother was diagnosed with breast cancer and long-term prognosis was not encouraging. Then Eloise came down with pancreatitis and spent a month in the hospital. Upon discharge, she was in bed at home for another three months and at reduced activity for another nine months. Unfortunately, when Ted quit the post office, he had given up health insurance; now he must pay hospital bills out of his wages.

Worries, added household burdens and medical expenses all began to weigh heavily on Ted, who was struggling with his own disabilities. To increase income, he worked more and traveled farther on sheep-shearing jobs. It was a pace he could not sustain.

Then more bad news. While shearing lambs in Emporia, Kansas, he heard Vicki had acute appendicitis. Ted left the job and hurried back in time to see Vicki after surgery. She recovered all right, but she would not be much help around the house for a while. Of course, another doctor bill was forthcoming.

Yet there was a fortuitous aspect to Vicki's illness. Ida May now took a turn for the worse and Ted was there for her last days. Night and day he spent a lot of time at his mother's bedside, and they conversed to the end. Religion was frequently a topic.

Ida May seldom had gone to church in her lifetime, but she was a Christian. Daughter Shirley opined her mother didn't attend services because she couldn't dress appropriately; Ida would never spend money on herself while she had daughters needing dresses, shoes and other necessities. Ida was also bothered by the hypocrisy of those who would pray on Sundays but carouse and philander the rest of the week.

Nonetheless, Ida May believed and "accepted Jesus Christ as her Lord and Savior." Ted recalled her last words: "Don't fret about me. I know where I'm going." She died peacefully and heroically on February 21, 1964, leaving a lasting void in the Charlie Sprouse family.

Ted suffered yet another loss that year. Since medical expenses were eating up most of his earnings, Ted defaulted on mortgage payments. Consequently, in late 1964 he was notified his house was being repossessed. What was he to do?

He also found worries in the larger context of the times. President John F. Kennedy had been assassinated at Thanksgiving in 1963 in what some suspected was an international plot. Kennedy had sent military advisers to Southeast Asia where "another Korea" seemed in the making. Already several American soldiers had died and others were missing in action, probably captured. Would the building international crisis be resolved before his sons—Steve and Rodney—became eligible for military service?

As Ted pondered the depressing scene, his chronic indigestion returned, his back pained more than ever, and his lower extremities hurt all the time. He couldn't work, feeling as he did. The challenges ahead seemed insurmountable.

When twelve-year-old Vicki went into the backyard one evening, she found her dad hiding in bushes near the end of the lot. Startled, she ran into the house to tell her mother.

Ted Sprouse was back in limbo.

XI
REMEDIATION

With Ted emotionally shot following chaotic 1964, Eloise showed resourcefulness and astuteness. She worked with Ted to sort out assets for something to build on. Basically, everyone was healthy again and willing to pitch in. Of immediate concern was a place to live.

Eloise talked to Uncle Willis Kratzer, who had an acreage on the Iowa side of the border near Lancaster, Missouri. The Sprouse's rented the place for $25 a month. Besides a modest house, the lot had space for a garden, orchard and chickens. Just what they needed to get started again.

Eloise set up a comfortable home. Ted planted a garden and nurtured apple and cherry trees to bear fruit. He raised chickens to supplement vegetables and fruit on the family menu. Eloise's parents had a lake in nearby Missouri, so Ted's family periodically went there to relax and fish. They dressed and froze the catch for the trip home. For cash income, Ted went back to shearing sheep when he was physically able. Thus they eked out a living and stabilized family finances.

Although Ida May was gone, survivors were adjusting well enough. Charlie and Kyle continued to live in the Drakesville home. Charlie kept up a brave front and still sheared sheep occasionally. Kyle, subject to periodic epileptic seizures, did odd jobs for Oren Jones, a long-time family friend. The girls had left home to work and marry. Don now was established in nearby Muscatine, where he worked for the local newspaper.

The year 1965 was one of promise and contentment, especially after Steve arrived for summer vacation. Eloise took a job in Centerville, and Vicki worked for Grandpa Brunk

133

selling firecrackers and at odd jobs. Rodney mowed lawns for neighbors and Steve tied hay bales for an enterprising farmer. At summer's end, the children had money to buy clothing for school and "something special."

In Steve's case, the special item was a bicycle, which he enjoyed riding over roads and paths nearby. When time came for Steve to return to Joanne and her second husband, Ted Evans, near Centerville, Steve put the bike in Sprouses' storage shed. After all, it was part of his Sprouse family— not his Evans family. Such compartmentalization came at an emotional cost, however.

The night before he left, Steve went outside to sit on the steps by himself. When Eloise went to talk to him, she found him crying. When asked why, Steve said he didn't want to leave <u>this</u> family.

"I've had a great time with all of you," he explained. "Already, I miss this place."

Between September and February, Steve came to visit several times, even though he was involved in high school activities. Always he enjoyed himself—until it was time to go back. This tugging of emotions concerned Ted, and he wondered what should be done about it. These should be stable years for a fifteen-year-old boy.

Of continuing concern was Ted's health. Shearing sheep was too strenuous as a day-in and day-out occupation. He gutted it out for a year or so, then reentered Veterans Hospital in February 1966. This time doctors operated to repair vertebrae damaged by that concussion grenade back in December 1950. Although surgery was successful, Ted lay on his back for a month and then wore a brace for another nine months. However, he was able to garden and tend chickens when he returned home. Eventually, his disability rating was increased to forty percent and the monthly check adjusted upward.

134

While Ted was in the hospital, Steve called Eloise and asked if he could ride with the family to visit his dad. Eloise said she would come by on the weekend and pick him up. However, on Friday night, Steve again called to say his mother would not let him go. The youth was crying, so Eloise asked to talk to Joanne.

"It won't do any good," Steve said and hung up.

When Eloise told Ted about this, he thought for a moment and then said, "This is tearing the kid apart. We're going to have to look closer at this whole arrangement."

They didn't see Steve again until he came for the summer. In the meantime, Ted talked to a lawyer. What about getting full custody of Steve? The lawyer opined that Steve's desires at sixteen would certainly weigh heavily on a judge's decision. At that point, Ted and Eloise agreed to let Steve decide.

As always, it was a pleasure having Steve there. He was pleasant, considerate and willing to lend a helping hand to his siblings and parents. He enjoyed bike riding, meeting people along the way, getting exercise. The summer sped by and the time for Steve to return to Centerville arrived.

They both talked to Steve, pointing out his options and reminding him that the trauma of switching back and forth was wrenching for all of them. Steve said the Evans had offered incentives for him to remain with them and work the farm. At sixteen, he was certainly able and qualified to do much of the farming. Upon departing, Steve said he wanted time to think the matter over. It seemed significant to Ted that Steve again stored his bike at the Sprouses.

Yet, Ted and Eloise were not sanguine about a change. For one thing, Steve was halfway through high school and it would be difficult for him to leave friends and activities at that point. Also, Ted was not sure what Joanne was telling

Steve about his father. The Sprouses were not surprised when they didn't hear from Steve right away, but they never thought it would be so long before they heard from him again.

As months passed, Ted and Eloise concluded that Steve had decided to stay with the Evans family. It was a disappointment, of course, but Ted believed even that choice was better than Steve's being jerked hither and yon. After all, Steve soon would be a young man and off on his own anyway.

Ted took consolation from the rest of his family. Eloise was always supportive, tolerant and loyal. Vicki was a joy, an energetic and attractive young lady. Rodney was a good student and a willing helper on the acreage. Indeed, Ted had much to be thankful for when he thought rationally rather than emotionally.

Of course, there was "the best friend a man ever had"—Don Cloud. They called each other frequently and occasionally sent letters back and forth. Cloud was adjusting, facilitated by the birth of two daughters. Still in the Army, he had advanced to Warrant Officer Instructor in communications. With a view toward retiring in the near future, he was looking for employment at Redstone Arsenal in Huntsville. Whenever they broke off a call or sent a note, both vowed to get together soon, real soon.

Even though his back bothered less than before, Ted knew his sheep-shearing days were numbered. Besides being too taxing, the craft provided low pay and no benefits. With his age creeping upward, Ted needed employment with health insurance and a retirement plan. Thus, he was receptive when a friend made an offer.

Elmer Jones worked for Critic Feeds based in Beardstown, Illinois. Elmer needed an assistant to help with sales out of Fairfield, Iowa. The job sounded promising, so Ted went for an interview and was accepted. In early 1967,

Ted rented a house at 409 North E Street and moved his family from the acreage to Fairfield, a city of some ten thousand. Ted's sales territory covered a fifty-mile radius around Fairfield. Critic Feeds provided a company car for Ted to make the rounds.

Selling was easier physically than sheep shearing and Ted earned an adequate wage. Compensation included health and retirement plans as well. However, Ted soon concluded he wasn't cut out to be a salesman; he had been a laborer all his life and he thrived on physical activity. Then, too, he saw little chance of advancement any time soon.

Since his family liked Fairfield and its people, Ted began looking there for something more suitable to earn a living. When Earl Perry's Sinclair service station came up for sale, Ted bought it on contract. He was familiar with servicing cars and dealing with customers, so he was confident he could make the venture pay. Eloise joined in as bookkeeper and assistant manager.

Together, they built up a sizable clientele by putting in long hours, providing good service at reasonable prices, and being accommodative. In fact, too accommodative. Ted towed and repaired cars on credit and wouldn't turn down anyone needing a tank of gas. By the time he and Eloise realized they were being too generous, it was too late.

"If I could have collected what people owed me, I would have been all right," Ted reflected.

As it was, Ted's creditors shut him down. He sold out but ended up with little compensation. He was in such a financial bind he took bankruptcy to protect personal property and essentials of livelihood.

Following a now-familiar pattern, Ted's health began to fail. In mid-1968 he returned to Veterans Hospital with recurring headaches, lightheadedness and occasional blackouts.

137

Ted Sprouse was back into mental depression and deeply distrustful of just about everyone.

During evaluation, doctors suspected a brain tumor and revealed as much to Eloise. "Don't tell him, though," they cautioned. "He's in no condition to handle bad news." Further tests proved negative, but Ted was to remain hospitalized for a while. Although direct medical costs were absorbed by Veterans Administration, Ted's illness was still costly to the family because of lost income.

Doctors operated to repair Ted's stomach lining and remove his gall bladder. He was given more psychiatric counseling so that he could grow to trust people again. After some three months, Ted Sprouse returned to Fairfield feeling better physically and in an improved state of mind.

As worshippers at Calvary Baptist Church now, the Sprouses prayed a lot. They were thankful, of course, but they needed help to escape financial doldrums. Somewhat meekly, Ted beseeched God to assist him once more. He needed a well-paying job in order to support his family and eventually buy a home. Shortly, an "angel" of a sort appeared.

Robert D. (Bob) Moore, Director of Public Works in Fairfield, dropped by to make an offer. How would Ted like to work for the city as streetsweeper? No broom nor trash can, of course, but he would operate a new motorized sweeper for $2.20 an hour, plus overtime. There would be health insurance and a retirement plan. Ted's prayers had been answered, and in November 1969 Ted became a city employee.

Although he believed God had helped him, Ted believed in helping himself from here on. Soon he not only operated the streetsweeper, but took on other tasks as well. Fixing lights, making minor street repairs, and assisting people in distress became part of Ted's routine. He had become convinced Fairfielders were a caring and friendly lot. Fast disappearing was Ted's lapse into paranoia.

As Vicki and Rodney matured, Eloise went to work at King's Grocery. It wasn't something she set out to do, but when manager Jerry King asked if she would help out temporarily as night checkout clerk Eloise said, "Yes." But as it happened, she liked the work, customers and hours and stayed on. It was a timely move, since they needed the money and Eloise enjoyed a change of routine.

With finances restored and everyone healthy and busy, the Sprouse family was reasonably secure. Even when Rodney tumbled from a ladder while painting the house and lacerated a kidney, bills were manageable. Rodney was hospitalized, had two ribs removed and spent nearly a year in recuperation. He eventually recovered but was unable to participate in contact sports afterwards. But there was still baseball.

Ted Sprouse's Fairfield Twins at the Iowa State Tournament, July 1968.

Ted became manager—he preferred being called "coach"—of a team in Babe Ruth baseball where Rodney was an enthusiastic competitor. Coaching included mealtime chats, as Rodney listened for tips that would help him improve. Ted also umpired on occasion, especially when a scheduled official failed to show. More and more he tended to regard sports as character builders rather than contests. In this respect, coaching and umpiring baseball had more and more appeal to Ted Sprouse.

Vicki graduated from Fairfield High School in 1971. She had an excellent student record and was certainly college qualified. However, Vicki was uncertain on several counts. First, she had found high school boring, unchallenging. Second, she didn't really know what she wanted to study. Third, there was the matter of paying for college. Lastly, she was dating Ron Palm, a Parsons College student. Ultimately, she went to work at King's Grocery, slipping into Eloise's job.

After two years with King's, Eloise had gone to work for Giant Grocery where she had daytime hours at a higher wage. The Sprouses needed all the income they could muster, for they purchased the house they had been renting. As homeowners, they had ascended another rung up the economic ladder.

The next year, Ted's father passed away. Charlie's death was not a surprise since his health had been failing steadily. Of course, Kyle, still at home, was most directly affected. He continued to live in the Drakesville house and to work for Oren Jones. When Oren died a couple years later, Kyle went to Quincey, Illinois, to live near his sister Betty. The Spouse Drakesville home—a shrine of so much family activity and nostalgia—had shut down.

It dawned on Ted one day that he hadn't heard from Don

Cloud in over a year. Sprouse had been so caught up in his own hectic affairs that he lost track of time. Wondering what his friend was up to, Ted called on the phone—and learned Cloud's number was unlisted! When a Christmas card went unanswered, Ted became concerned. Through Veterans Affairs he obtained the address of a locator service in St. Louis. Ted sent a note for forwarding to Don Cloud—wherever he might be. Encouraging for Sprouse, he had come upon no indication that Cloud was not alive and well.

Ted Sprouse and his grandson, Daniel Palm, 4, at a Christmas decoration ceremony in 1976 in Fairfield, Iowa.

Then Ted reflected on his life. He liked his job with the city and he was earning a good living. They had purchased a home with manageable mortgage payments and were building equity. Eloise was healthy and enjoying her work with Giant Grocery. Vicki had married Ron Palm in 1972 and they were expecting their first child. Rodney was part-time manager at "Dads and Lads," a Fairfield clothing store, even while still a high school student. He planned to attend college eventually. As for Steve, they now accepted his alienation; Ted and Eloise had done the right thing in simplifying his life.

Ted himself again trusted people—even those outside the family circle. Somehow—despite more than his share of ups and downs—Ted Sprouse had landed on his feet. It was a good feeling to be standing tall once again.

XII
FREE AT LAST!

Promotion to Street Superintendent in 1979 helped convince Ted that he had finally "escaped," that he had shaken the POW syndrome that had entrapped him. He now had real responsibilities and earned a respectable salary. Obviously, his superiors had been impressed with his work, and just about everyone around liked Ted Sprouse.

Ted had so many involvements he barely had an idle moment. He umpired baseball and softball games several times a week. He called games at the state softball tournaments in both Fairfield and Ottumwa. He umpired for Parsons College and independent baseball teams throughout southeastern Iowa. He was paid twenty-five dollars a game, but money was just part of the compensation. Ted enjoyed returning to the "one big recreation of his life."

Although his feet and legs were often painful, especially in cold weather, the condition was by no means disabling. Ted went to work every day—whatever the weather. However, another health problem eventually caught up with him.

Recurring chest pains back in 1977 had sent Ted to Fairfield Hospital for a check up. Suspecting a heart condition, doctors transferred Ted to Methodist Teaching Hospital in Des Moines. An angiogram disclosed occluding arteries, so he was given medication and told to avoid stress as much as possible. But Ted had a job to do, so he couldn't ease up much at the time.

After initial improvement, the symptoms returned. Ted reentered Methodist Hospital in 1980 for an angioplasty—the balloon treatment. Two weeks later he returned to his job with renewed zest. Ted's out-of-pocket costs were manageable—thanks to the city's employee health plan.

When Don Cloud received Ted's note forwarded by Army Retired Activities, he called and suggested they get together. Would Ted and Eloise come for a visit to Huntsville? Cloud reminded Ted that almost thirty years had gone by since they had last seen each other in Drakesville shortly after their return from Korea. Ted decided not to delay any longer, so he and Eloise took vacation time in June 1984 and drove to Huntsville.

Ted Sprouse (left) and Don Cloud in Huntsville, Alabama, June, 1984.

After retiring from the Army in the mid-1960s, Cloud had gone to work for National Aeronautices and Space Agency (NASA) in Huntsville. He also continued college by attending off-duty classes under the GI Bill. After years of persistence, Don Cloud was awarded a degree in electrical engineering. With the added credential, Cloud was promoted to a highly responsible position in classified space operations.

Because of the nature of his duties, he had become inaccessible in some respects—the unlisted phone number, for example. Thus, he had lost touch with Ted Sprouse over the years.

Sprouse was not surprised at Cloud's success. "He was the smartest guy I ever knew," Ted recalled. "And he was very dedicated."

The three-day visit revolved around reminiscing. They would go on short drives around Huntsville and out for lunch or dinner, but the central activity was conversation between Don Cloud and Ted Sprouse. Both Eloise and Freddie, Cloud's wife, listened with considerable interest throughout.

Eloise already had heard much of what the men talked about, but Freddie had heard little previously. In a moment of candor, she said to Eloise, "I'm glad you folks are here. Don won't talk to me about his prisoner experiences, but I wish that he would. Maybe then I would have understood what he was going through those first years after he came back."

Cloud was pleased to hear that Ted had finally righted himself—and he was not surprised. "Ted is as solid as they come," he confided to Eloise. "If it hadn't been for him I would not have survived prison camp."

Eloise was struck by the words; they were exactly those used by her husband to describe his indebtedness to Don Cloud. Both men were right, of course.

Ted and Eloise had rented a motel nearby. They talked long into the night about the day's happenings. Unexpectedly, Eloise said, "I don't know why you two get along so well. Don's educated, articulate and such a go-getter. Sometimes I think you two have little in common."

"I've wondered about that, too," Ted replied. "And it's funny that we hit it off. One thing, though, we always trusted each other. We both have values like religion, loyalty and

144

sense of responsibility. And don't forget I always came through for Don when he needed me."

"I'm sure you did, Ted."

A highlight of the visit came on the last night, when Cloud presented Ted with an eight-by-ten glossy photo of Camp 5 taken by satellite from outer space. "Just in case you ever yearn for the good old days, look at this," Cloud said wryly.

Don Cloud and "Freddie" at the time of Sprouse's visit to Huntsille, Alabama, June, 1984.

With wives looking on, Ted and Don identified hooches and landmarks on the sharply detailed photo. Missing, of course, was the "ambiance" that had made Pyoktong a prison in every sense of the word. "The picture is sterile," Cloud pointed out. "No smells, no lice, no wet, no cold, no pain, no time—no endless, endless time."

Back in Fairfield, Ted and Eloise became involved with activities of their offspring. Ron and Vicki Palm had moved to Oskaloosa in 1982 when Ron went to work for Farm Service there. With their two children now in school, Vicki enrolled in Indian Hills Community College in Ottumwa. She sailed through academics and was awarded an Associate Nursing Degree in 1985. Ambitions heightened, she enrolled in University of Missouri, St. Louis, on her way to the Bachelor's Degree as a nurse practitioner. In the meantime, she gave birth to Nathan Andrew in 1987.

Rodney attended Bob Jones University in South Carolina for a couple years, but he became disenchanted with the curriculum and returned to Fairfield. He met Gloria Roberts from Keosauqua, Iowa, and they married in 1982. Gloria had a daughter from a previous marriage and she and Rodney added a boy and girl of their own.

As for Steve, a friend of Eloise in Centerville occasionally furnished a bit of news. After graduation from high school in 1969, Steve had joined the Marine Corps and served in Vietnam. Upon discharge from the Marines four years later, he eventually worked for Young Radiator in Centerville. He married Marlene Stanton in 1980 and they had a son, Beau. However, Ted still heard nothing directly from Steve.

When Bob Moore died suddenly in November 1986, Ted Sprouse was promoted to Superintendent of Public Works. He now supervised street, sewer, airport and traffic maintenance. He had nine employees and several items of heavy equipment to oversee. His annual budget was over five-million dollars. Although the pace was hectic at times, Ted handled it readily.

"I had good workers and good customers, which made it all very satisfying," he recalled later.

On the spur of the moment in 1986, Ted decided to invite the Clouds for a visit. Don said he couldn't get away, but they would be happy to entertain the Sprouses again in Huntsville. So Ted and Eloise headed south once more.

Without a doubt, Cloud was a very busy man, for the visit was interrupted several times by phone calls and Cloud was called once to the NASA facility. Still, they were able to reminisce a couple days and spend time with the Cloud daughters, who were both in college. They were intelligent, courteous and attractive young ladies. Obviously, they had been well brought up, thanks to loving, caring parents.

When he was discharged from the Army in 1953, Ted Sprouse had paid scant attention to awards due him. In fact, he couldn't recall if the subject even came up. Thirty years later, however, the head of the local chapter of Disabled American Veterans mentioned the oversight in conversation with Ted one day. Ted was lukewarm at first, but he respected Colonel Bob Robinson who offered to help. Robinson, a veteran with twenty-nine years in the Army Judge Advocate Corps, sent a query to Army Records Administration in 1984.

Some four years later, the official response reached Fairfield, Iowa. An advisory suggested the enclosed decorations be awarded to Sprouse at an appropriate ceremony. Several possibilities were offered, but Sprouse insisted upon Robinson doing the honors.

Colonel Robinson mustered a band and local officials for a fitting presentation. On September 11, 1988, some 250 veterans, co-workers and citizens gathered in Fairfield Central Park in late afternoon. The 34th Army Band played martial music and patriotic songs. Two local vocalists, Jan Hunterdose and Lee Ann Lantz, sang "God Bless America" to introduce the occasion.

Colonel Robinson welcomed guests and honorees. He reminded those gathered that Ted Sprouse's "ordeal had not ended merely because the gates to freedom were thrown open. But the same courage and conviction that enabled Ted Sprouse to survive his captivity continued to serve him and sustain him throughout that critical period of readjustment and continued survival."

Mayor Robert Rasmussen spoke for the city in paying tribute. He concluded with: "Very few of Ted Sprouse's coworkers ever were aware of the stress, the turmoil he experienced in serving his country. Citizens of this city are better off that Ted did not give up."

Colonel Robinson then pinned ribbons for the United Nations Service Medal, Republic of Korea Presidential Unit Citation, Korean Service Medal with ten battle stars, National Defense Service Medal, Good Conduct Medal, Purple Heart, and Prisoner of War Medal on Ted Sprouse's navy blue blazer. Visibly moved, Ted returned to his seat beside Eloise without speaking. His silence made what followed all the more touching.

Ted Spouse being aswarded medals for Korean service in September 1988 by Colonel Bob Robinson, USA, Ret.

Rodney had been asked to say a few words in his father's behalf. Rodney had difficulty composing a formal speech, so he spoke extemporaneously:

> I've never been in Korea, or in Vietnam. But I've seen Korea in my father's eyes—many times. I've seen my father conquer Korea years after that conflict ended—the memories, the sufferings, the fears.
>
> I'm thankful for what his generation did—the dedication and patriotism they displayed. I hope my generation has learned about patriotism from him. I hope we would be up to similar challenges. For that I'm grateful.

When his voice quavered, Rodney broke off and walked over to embrace his father.

The ceremony closed with the *Star Spangled Banner*; Ted Sprouse's Korean wartime service had been validated—thirty-five years after the fact. In a favorable twist, the event had been timely—most timely.

Ted and Eloise Sprouse and their family following the Korean War medal presentation in Fairfield, Iowa, September 11, 1988.

149

News accounts accompanied by photos circulated via regional newspapers. Steve Sprouse read the story in his daily paper, every word of it. He scanned pictures more than once. He glanced at son Beau who had never met his grandfather, had never seen him, had never heard his voice. Had Beau been shortchanged because of Steve's decision nearly twenty-three years ago?

Steve mailed a Christmas card to Ted and Eloise that year. He included a picture of Beau. He wrote a few words on the card, saying he would like for them to meet their grand-son when it was convenient. In such fashion, the long es-trangement between father and son ended.

Within a short while, Steve, his wife Marlene and son Beau drove to Fairfield. Understandably, the meeting was a bit awkward. Nonetheless, the ice had been broken. Ted and Eloise liked Marlene from the start. Of course, Beau was ev-erything they thought he might be—a handsome grandson. Steve tried hard to avoid unpleasantness of any sort; there-fore, nothing of the past ever came up. Nor would it in years to come. The important thing, of course, was that Ted had regained a son and gained a daughter-in-law and a grandson.

Although Ted had welcomed added responsibilities in his job, stress took its toll. In years following the angioplasty, Ted had two more episodes of chest pains. When symptoms again became acute in late 1989, he went back to his cardi-ologist. Blood clots were found in Ted's lung and coronary arteries. Immediate rest and medication were prescribed to clear the clots, but the doctor advised stress avoidance as the best therapy.

With no choice remaining, Ted submitted his resigna-tion as Public Works Superintendent in January 1990. He told city officials, "I have mixed emotions about leaving the job, but I just know it has to be this way."

Ted Sprouse as Superintendant of Public Works, Fairfield, Iowa, 1988

Mayor Rasmussen and City Administrator John F. Brown not only expressed regrets, but they issued a public statement of appreciation and arranged for a plaque in recognition of Ted's twenty-one years of dedicated service to the people of Fairfield.

Ted Sprouse's heart condition improved encouragingly; he had done the right thing. And he now had time for gardening, traveling and his seven grandchildren. But Ted had not dropped entirely out of sight on the Fairfield scene. He was asked to be featured speaker at Fairfield Memorial Day Ceremony on May 31st, 1993. The suggested topic was "Heroes."

In assembling his thoughts, Ted Sprouse reflected on all the courageous people he had known in the Army, prison camps, sports, American history and everyday life. Of all those he had met in his sixty-six years, one ranked above all others. Ted's remarks on that sun-filled day in Central Park were brief—but they revealed the soul of the man:

Heroes. A perfect topic on this day set aside in memory of those who have given so much for each and everyone of us. We've all heard of famous heroes from our different wars, but I want to talk to you about rarely mentioned heroes.

The one I want to tell you about was born July 22, 1900, and she died February 21, 1964. Her name: Ida May Sprouse. At age eighteen she first experienced the cost of war. Her brother died while serving in World War I. How could she have guessed that she was being prepared for other losses to be endured in years to come.

It has been said that the most traumatic tragedy parents may face is when they outlive a child. I am sure my mother would have agreed on that horrible day she received news that her son, Rex, had died while serving our country in World War II. A week earlier she had received word Rex was "missing in action." If only that had been true! Even after she received official notice that Rex was dead, she did not give up. For five eternally long and painful years she hoped and prayed that somehow, somewhere her son was still alive—that he was just "missing in action."

After I joined the Army in 1949, I learned how and where my brother had died—and where he was buried. News that death came quickly to Rex and knowing where his remains were laid to rest brought mother some peace. But that peace was short lived, for I was taken prisoner by the Chinese in December of 1950. For an entire year, my mother again suffered the anguish of a son "missing in action."

In the thirty-three months I remained a prisoner of war, I witnessed great acts of heroism and courage amidst unmentionable pain and suffering. The first year alone, 1600 men died in prison camp. In fact, 61% of my comrades died in prison camp before our release in September 1953.

Even though I was with some of the bravest and most courageous people I have ever known, not one was braver nor more courageous than my mother. Unwavering and faithful in prayer, she awaited my return.

152

So, on this day set aside to pay special tribute to those brave and courageous men and women who have faithfully served our country abroad, let us not forget loved ones back home who prayerfully and faithfully awaited return of sons and daughters. And let us pay special tribute to mothers and fathers whose sons and daughters never returned home—whose remains rest in far away cemeteries and watery graves around the world.

I thank God for this great country and the brave people who loved it enough to sacrifice everything and anything so that we all can be free. My earnest prayer is that we will always be free and that we not only say "In God We Trust," but practice "In God We Trust."

"Trust" was high on Ted Sprouse's list of personal qualities. He had seen the tragic consequences of character lapses in wartime and in peacetime. As he—in effect—reminded Eloise before they married, "If there is no trust, there is no future."

Perhaps succeeding generations will learn about patriotism from Ted Sprouse, for Ted was unabashedly patriotic. He truly believed he lived in the best country in the world and certainly the freest. Ted Sprouse appreciated freedom as few man can—and at last he was free! Thanks to God, a loyal comrade, a loving family, a caring community, and his own dogged persistence.

EPILOGUE

The Korean Conflict was an abrupt switch in the way we fight wars, and Teddy R. Sprouse became a hapless pawn in the new paradigm. For the first time, Americans fought unscrupulous communists on the battlefield—an experience for which they were ill-prepared. For the first time, the United States fought a limited war—the risk of nuclear war was too great to do otherwise. For the first time, we fended off an enemy's proxy while we forced communist ideologues in Moscow to compound insoluble problems at home.

In the long term the approach worked and four decades later communism collapsed resoundingly. In the short term, however, the outcome was anything but neat, and a half century later we still deal with its remnants. Technically, a state of war still exists in Korea.

The peninsula remains divided, dangerous and controversial. Some 37,000 American servicemen—many are grandchildren of men who fought there—remain to help the Republic of Korea military guard against another attack from the north. Some 8,100 Americans remain unaccounted for, including 389 once listed as prisoners of war. And we remain largely ignorant of Korea's painful legacy, a shortsightedness that led to our becoming entangled in Vietnam a decade later.

Some Americans questioned the performance of those who fought in Korea. Especially disillusioning were tales of American prisoners cooperating with their captors. "Brainwashing" was a puzzling term and Americans had difficulty in accepting the results. Postwar studies were to show that most prisoners went along with indoctrination sessions as a way of surviving. Many signed peace petitions and pro-communist testimonials to signal folks back home they were alive and well. However, most shied away from saying anything clearly traitorous. Of course, there were the twenty-one who refused repatriation, an unacceptable act by any American.

Hastily, Americans concluded "Korea was the first war we lost." Some concluded the expenditure in lives (33,629 died), trauma and resources had not been worth the coin.

With doubts and no clear-cut victory, Americans as a whole turned away from the Korean War quickly—too quickly—and went on to more pleasant things in their busy and affluent lives. Following the consensus, government officials likewise tended to brush the unpopular war aside.

In the midst of pervasive cynicism, Korean ex-prisoners also were brushed aside. Professional help, treatment facilities and prescriptions for rehabilitation were inadequate and insufficient by most standards of fairness. The severely traumatized, such as Ted Sprouse, should have been singled out for special and extended treatment. Obviously they had serious physical problems due to enemy action, deprivation of essentials and exposure to harsh elements. Less obvious but more profound were psychological problems—paranoia and insecurities that continued to overwhelm them.

Ted Sprouse deserved more empathy than he received, but, of course, post-traumatic stress disorder (PTSD) was not an acceptable affliction at the time. Because his needs were ignored, Ted Sprouse's "second war was worse than the first." This time those near him suffered, too. Ultimately, Ted Sprouse was salvaged and, remarkably, he harbors no bitterness.

Teddy R. Sprouse had been fated to undertake a Homeric journey through limbo on the Yalu River and the netherworld beyond. Indeed, the Fates scarcely could have elected a more disinclined protagonist to serve as hero. Yet, it must be said in retrospect that he displayed the best of human traits throughout his odyssey.

BACKGROUND

1. Appleman, Roy E. *South to the Naktong, North to the Yalu*. (U.S. Army in the Korean War Series) Office of Military History, Dept. of Army, Wash, D.C. 1961. Reprint 1973.

2. Blair, Clay. *The Forgotten War*. (America in Korea 1950-1953) An Anchor Press Book by Doubleday. New York, London, Toronto, Sydney, Aukland. 1987.

3. Kinkead, Eugene, *In Every War But One*. W. W. Norton & Co., Inc. New York. 1959.

4. Rees, David. *Korea: The Limited War*. St. Martin's Press. New York. 1964.

5. Spurr, Russell. *Enter the Dragon*. New Market Press. New York. 1988.

6. Stokesbury, James L. *Short History of the Korean War*. William Morrow and Co., Inc. New York. 1988.

7. Summers, Harry G., Jr. *Korean War Almanac*. Facts on File. New York, Oxford, Sydney. 1990.

Photo by Tom Jacoby

About the author:

Colonel Robert J. Berens retired in 1977 after 32 years of army service. As an enlisted man he participated in the 1942 invasion of North Africa and the Tunisian and Italian campaigns. He was also a platoon leader in Korea and the information officer of II Corps in Vietnam in 1969. Since retiring from military service, he teaches written communications at the college level and writes defense-related articles for professional magazines.

Wishing you a very
Merry
Christmas

Sprouse
1953